MW01532685

Following Directions and Aural Reasoning
Pre-Kindergarten to Second Grade

Written and published by: Bright Kids NYC

Copyright © 2012 by Bright Kids NYC Inc. All of the questions in this book have been created by the staff and consultants of Bright Kids NYC Inc.

The *Otis-Lennon School Ability Test®* (OLSAT®) is a registered trademark of NCS Pearson, Inc. The *Cognitive Abilities Test (CogAT®)* and the *Iowa Tests of Basic Skills® (ITBS®)* are registered trademarks of Houghton Mifflin Harcourt. Pearson Inc. and Houghton Mifflin Harcourt neither endorse nor support the content of the Bright Kids NYC Following Directions and Aural Reasoning workbook.

All rights reserved. No part of this book may be reproduced or transmitted in any form or by any means without written permission from the author. ISBN (978-1-935858-81-2)

Corporate Headquarters:
Bright Kids NYC Inc.
225 Broadway
Suite 1504
New York, NY 10007

www.brightkidsnyc.com
info@brightkidsnyc.com
917-539-4575

Table of Contents

5   About Bright Kids NYC

7   Introduction

9   Verbal Reasoning Subsections

11   How To Use This Book

13   Skill Builder Activities

25   Skill Builder Riddles

57   Aural Directions

81   Treasure Maps

95   Following Directions

127   Aural Reasoning

139   Answer Keys

Following Directions and Aural Reasoning

Bright Kids NYC Inc ©

About Bright Kids NYC

Bright Kids NYC was founded in New York City to provide language arts and math enrichment for young children. Our goal is to prepare students of all ages for standardized exams through assessments, tutoring workshops, and our publications. Our philosophy is that, regardless of age, test taking is a skill that can be acquired and mastered through practice.

At Bright Kids NYC, we strive to provide the best learning materials. Our publications are truly unique. All of our books have been created by qualified psychologists, learning specialists, teachers, and staff writers. Our books have also been tested by hundreds of children in our tutoring practice. Since children can make associations that many adults cannot, testing of materials by children is a critical step towards creating successful test preparation guides. Finally, our learning specialists and teaching staff have provided practical strategies and tips to help students compete successfully on standardized exams.

Feel free to contact us if you have any questions.

Corporate Headquarters:
Bright Kids NYC Inc.
225 Broadway
Suite 1504
New York, NY 10007

www.brightkidsnyc.com
info@brightkidsnyc.com
917-539-4575

Following Directions and Aural Reasoning Bright Kids NYC Inc ©

Introduction

Every year, thousands of young children in the United States take standardized tests required by their school systems for classroom placements, school readiness evaluations, and for entry into gifted and talented programs. Many of these standardized exams have questions that require a student to use his or her listening skills to determine the correct answer.

If your child is taking the OLSAT® Level A test, then he or she will encounter following directions and aural reasoning questions that are read by an administrator. Following directions questions asses a student's ability to select a representation that corresponds to the verbal description that was read out loud. Aural reasoning questions test the student's ability to visualize a situation, integrate appropriate details, and synthesize what has been described.

Other standardized exams use similar types of questions to test a student's verbal reasoning skills. The *CogAT®* Levels 5/6 and 7 use picture analogies, sentence completion, and picture classification questions to test a student's ability to understand oral vocabulary and sentence construction. The verbal sections on the *ITBS®* Levels 5 and 6 are orally administered tests that require a student to select an answer based on inferences and the student's background knowledge of the meanings of words.

The key element tested across all of these exams is the student's ability to use his or her listening skills, vocabulary, and knowledge of the world to select the correct visual representation. The Bright Kids NYC Following Directions and Aural Reasoning workbook for students in Pre-Kindergarten to Second Grade is designed to help your child better understand these concepts as he or she goes through the book. If your child is going to take the OLSAT®, *CogAT®*, or the *ITBS®*, then he or she will need to get used to solving the types of problems found in this book. We also recommend that you purchase our Arithmetic Reasoning workbook for students in Pre-Kindergarten to First Grade if your child struggles with listening and answering spoken mathematical word problems.

It is recommended that you work through this book with your child in a neutral environment free of noise and clutter. A comfortable seating arrangement will also help your child focus and concentrate to the best of his or her ability.

Most students will have to take numerous standardized exams throughout their school years. A good way to develop the critical thinking skills for these types of exams is to practice with similarly styled questions that test the core concepts found on the exams. This method helps ensure that a student will succeed on his or her exam.

Following Directions and Aural Reasoning

Bright Kids NYC Inc ©

Verbal Reasoning Subsections

Verbal skills are centered on a student's ability to listen carefully, follow directions, and understand vocabulary through receptive language. While verbal sections do require verbal knowledge, the multiple-choice options for most standardized exams on these sections are given in a visual form. In order to succeed on the verbal reasoning/listening sections of standardized exams, students must be able to accurately perceive and recall what has been perceived, understand patterns and relationships, use logical reasoning to deal with abstract items, and apply generalizations to new and different contexts.

Following Directions

The purpose of these questions is first and foremost to evaluate a student's listening skills. Following directions questions on the OLSAT® are utilized to assess a child's ability to apply relational concepts when finding the correct answer to pictorial and figural representations. Students must be attentive, listen carefully to the question, use short-term memory, and understand the relational vocabulary used in the questions. Following directions questions are only repeated once, unless it is specified in the instructions that the question may be repeated if necessary.

These concepts are commonly tested on following directions questions:

- Relational and directional vocabulary
- The meaning and use of conjunctions
- Ordinal numbers and words of degree
- Basic shapes
- Numbers and letters
- Magnitude and size

Aural Reasoning

Aural reasoning questions are also used on standardized exams to test a student's listening skills and his or her understanding of language and logic. On the OLSAT®, these questions require a student to understand the scenario that is being read out loud and to predict the outcome or deduce the logical result of the situation presented. Students must listen carefully to the scenario in order to comprehend and visualize the main idea and details of the situation.

These concepts are commonly tested on aural reasoning questions:

- General knowledge of the world
- Logical outcomes of different types of processes or actions
- Relational scenarios
- Short-term remembrance of details

How to Use This Book

The best way to use this book is to go through it question by question with your child. You should sit next to him or her and point to each question as you both move down the page. The most important thing to remember is to read the questions out loud to your child. You should also tell him or her to focus on the answer choices as you read the question out loud. In the early questions in each section, your child may need to hear the question more than once. However, as you move through each chapter, you should gradually work towards only reading the question once.

Make sure that your child is listening to the question when you read it out loud. You may want to repeat the phrase "Are you listening?" at points to make certain he or she is paying attention. If your child is having trouble focusing, consider using positive reinforcements to help him or her finish the questions in a particular chapter.

Try not to overwork your child by doing more than one chapter per day. While he or she should get used to doing a number of these questions in a row, you don't want your child to actively dislike these listening activities; his or her concentration is an important factor in whether he or she correctly understands the question. However, you also need to judge when he or she needs encouragement and a little extra push to finish a group of questions. Most standardized exams for Kindergarten and First Grade entry are over thirty minutes long, so a young student needs to get used to sitting still and concentrating for that amount of time or longer.

The chapters in this book generally progress by level of difficulty. The first two chapters contain skill builder activities that will help your child adjust to the types of listening questions found on standardized exams. The first chapter has activities that involve the aural and visual recognition of shapes, colors and their spatial relation within a row to one another. The second chapter has activities that require the student to recognize certain real-world qualities that are associated with various objects, figures, or pictures.

The questions in the third and fourth chapters focus on identifying scenarios, finding objects or recognizing certain actions in pictures, and distinguishing similar pictures from one another. The questions in the fifth chapter of this workbook focus on the student's ability to select the object that represents the description that was read out loud. These questions contain three levels to each question and each level increases in difficulty. You should go through each question in the chapter focusing on one level at a time until you have completed that level for every question in the chapter. The last chapter in this workbook focuses on questions that require a student to integrate important details into a spoken scenario and to synthesize what has been described in order to determine the most logical answer to the question.

Tips and Strategies

The most difficult aspect of verbal reasoning questions for children is recalling the spoken information in order to select the correct answer. When practicing these questions with your child, keep in mind that during formal testing, examiners are NOT allowed to repeat the question.

The following tips and strategies will be beneficial in helping your child with the material found in this section:

- Be conscious of how often you repeat the instructions to your child.

- If your child is a visual learner, ask him or her to visualize the spoken information and then match his or her own visualization with the answer choices.

- Ask your child to repeat the questions in a "whisper voice" so that he or she can remember and recall what is being said. The verbalization of what he or she heard can help illuminate the correct answer to the question.

- Make sure that your child is looking at all the answer choices while listening to the questions.

- If your child forgets part of the question, encourage him or her to choose an answer based on whatever he or she can remember about the question.

- The mental repetition of certain phrases in the question can help a student select the correct answer. This strategy can work particularly well with questions that require the student to remember the spatial relationships between various figures or objects in pictures.

- Encourage your child to use the process of elimination if he or she can definitely determine that one or more answer choices are clearly wrong.

- Your child may find it easier to recognize when there are different or the same types of objects mentioned in a question. For example, if a question asks the student to mark under the picture that shows a white, gray, and black dog, he or she may recognize that the correct answer will have dogs with three different colors. Any picture showing two dogs of the same color must be wrong. Thus, the student can use the process of elimination to narrow down the answer choices in the question.

- Some verbal reasoning questions require the student to relate a spoken scenario to a real-world result. If your child has problems with these questions, you should mention similar scenarios to help him or her understand the qualities associated with certain objects.

- When your child has answered every question in this book, you can still use the pictures in each question to come up with similar questions on your own.

Chapter One

Skill Builder Activities

25. Point to the figure that is a green rectangle next to a red rectangle.

26. Point to the figure that is a yellow circle next to a green circle.

27. Point to the figure that is a purple star next to a green rectangle.

28. Point to the figure that is a blue circle next to a two purple circles.

17. Point to the green spiral next to a blue diagonal line.

18. Point to the figure that is a red with four intersecting a red diagonal line.

19. Point to the figure that is blue diagonal line next to a red diagonal line.

20. Point to the figure that is a dark blue spiral square next to a red spiral.

Following Directions and Aural Reasoning Bright Kids NYC Inc ©

01. Point to the yellow circle that is next to a purple circle.

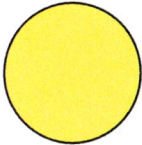

02. Point to the red square that is next to a yellow rectangle.

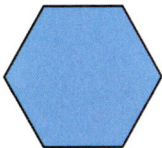

03. Point to the shape that is a yellow triangle next to a red square.

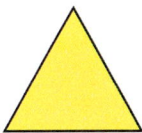

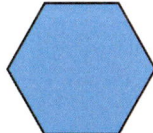

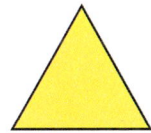

04. Point to the red circle that is next to a yellow rectangle.

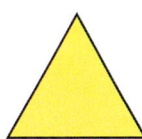

05. Point to the downward pointing red arrow that is next to a blue arrow.

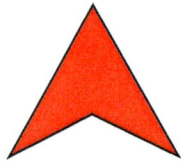

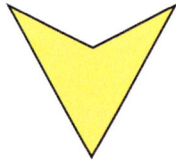

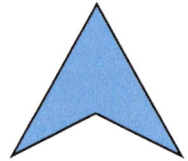

06. Point to the pink triangle that is next to a blue triangle.

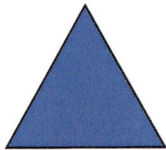

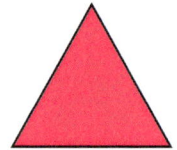

07. Point to the two yellow circles that are next to a blue square.

08. Point to the shape that has five corners and is next to a blue triangle.

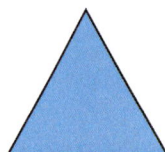

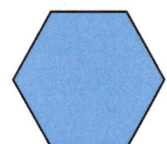

09. Point to the green line that is next to a purple straight line.

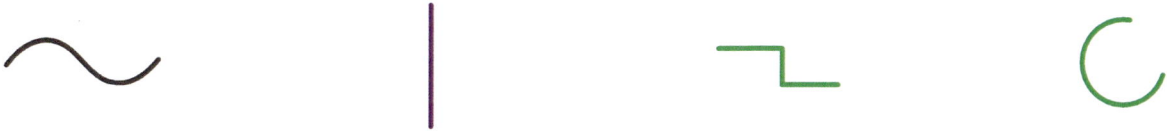

10. Point to the green zigzag line that is in between two red zigzag lines.

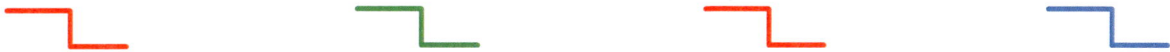

11. Point to the blue semicircle that is in between two red semicircles.

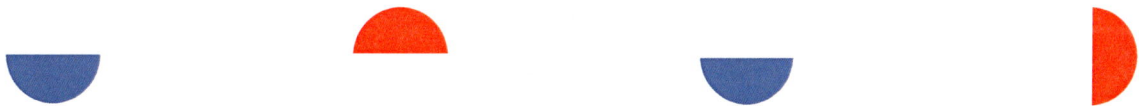

12. Point to the red curved line that is in between two purple straight lines.

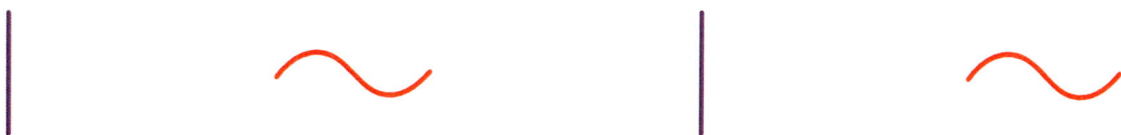

13. Point to the blue circle that is next to a purple diagonal line.

14. Point to the first plus sign that is purple.

15. Point to the shape that has the most sides and is next to a red circle.

16. Point to the green shape that is next to a green circle.

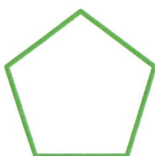

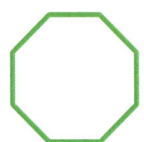

17. Point to the green rectangle that is next to a red rectangle.

18. Point to the yellow circle that is next to a green circle.

19. Point to the purple star that is next to a green rectangle.

20. Point to the blue circle that is next to two purple circles.

21. Point to the green zigzag line that is next to a red zigzag line.

22. Point to the purple line that is next to a green curved line.

23. Point to the green semicircle that is next to a red semicircle.

24. Point to the purple straight line that is next to a purple curved line.

Following Directions and Aural Reasoning   Bright Kids NYC Inc ©

25. **Point to the dark blue triangle that is next to a yellow arrow.**

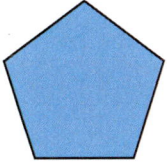

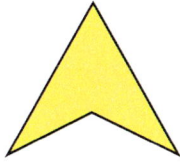

- -

26. **Point to the yellow circle that is next to a red triangle.**

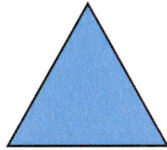

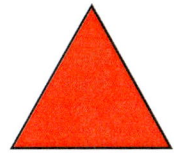

- -

27. **Point to the blue triangle that is next to an orange circle.**

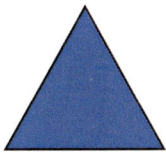

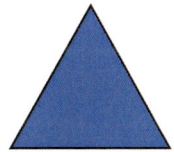

- -

28. **Point to the yellow arrow that is pointing up and is next to a green arrow that is also pointing up.**

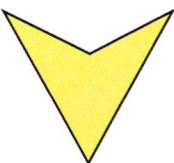

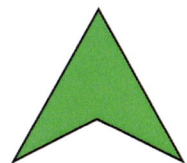

29. Point to the blue square that is next to a purple circle.

30. Point to the yellow rectangle that is next to a yellow triangle.

31. Point to the red square that is next to an orange triangle.

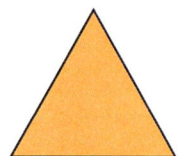

32. Point to the blue circle that is next to a red circle.

33. **Point to the green spiral that is next to a blue diagonal line.**

34. **Point to the purple diagonal line that is next to the plus sign.**

35. **Point to the blue diagonal line that is next to a red diagonal line.**

36. **Point to the blue spiral that is next to a red spiral.**

37. **Point to the shape that has two intersecting lines that are in between two blue shapes.**

38. **Point to the shape that is blue and red with four intersecting lines and is next to a red shape with four intersecting lines.**

39. **Point to the green horizontal line that is next to a blue diagonal line.**

40. **Point to the red shape with five intersecting lines that is next to a blue shape with four intersecting lines.**

Chapter Two

Skill Builder Activities
Riddles

15. Bird and a bear

together near a chair

Of the picture you see, which one is me?

11. I love to camp.

I started a fire and lit a lamp.

Of the pictures that you see, which one is

Following Directions and Aural Reasoning

Bright Kids NYC Inc ©

01. I am the color of grass in the park,

a very sour apple, or a frog sitting on a tree bark.

Of the pictures that you see, can you find me?

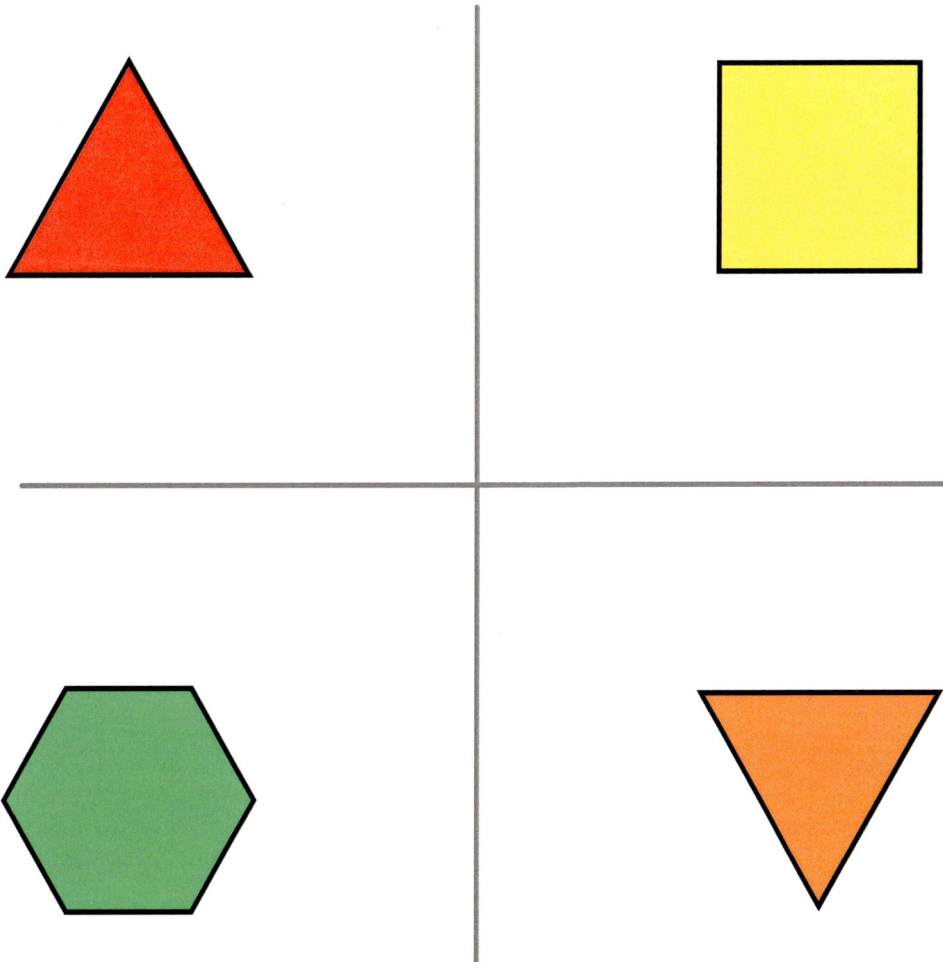

02. My favorite color is red.

My sister's is blue.

Mix the two, and you get this hue.

Of the pictures you see, which color is me?

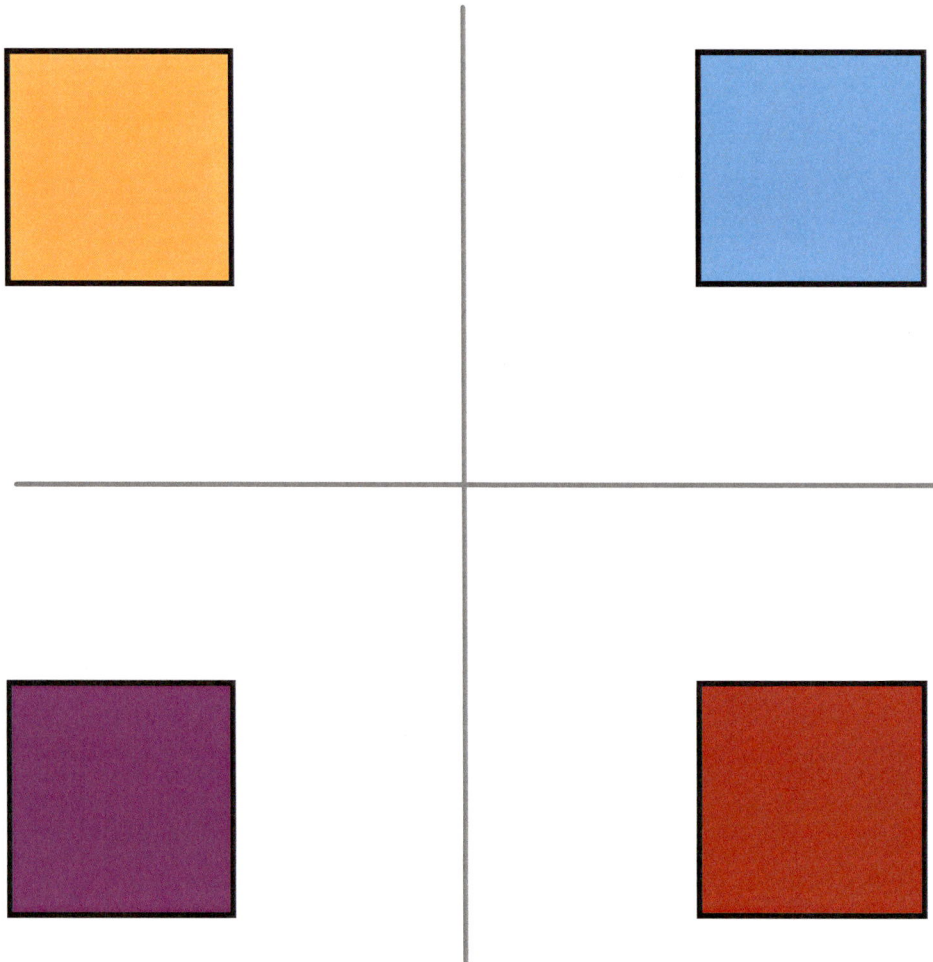

Following Directions and Aural Reasoning Bright Kids NYC Inc ©

03. I am bright at night.

You can see me without a light.

Of the pictures you see, which one is me?

04. I am like a moon.

I am like a ball.

I am the roundest one of all.

Of the pictures you see, which one is me?

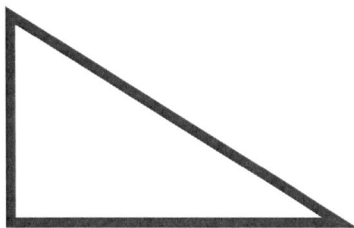

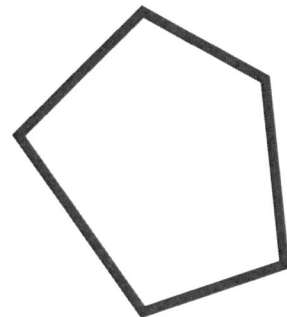

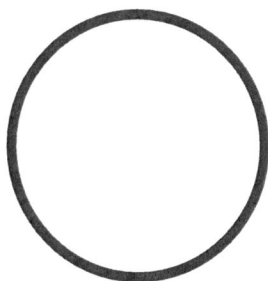

Following Directions and Aural Reasoning Bright Kids NYC Inc ©

05. I am round and half of me is green.

The other half is the darkest color you've ever seen.

Of the pictures you see, which one is me?

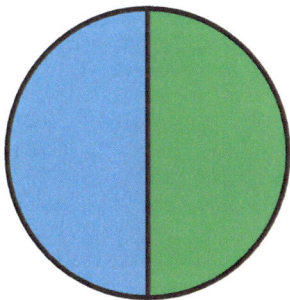

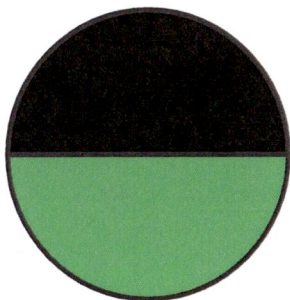

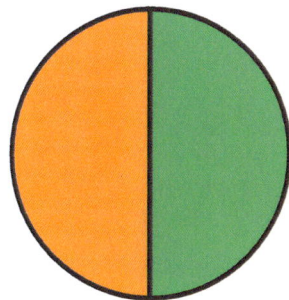

06. Many of me make a soccer ball.

I have more corners than all.

Of the pictures you see, can you find me?

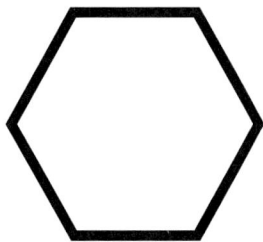

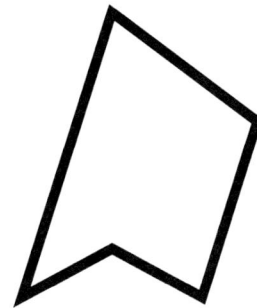

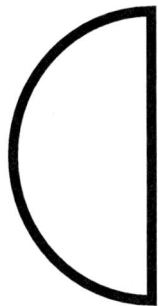

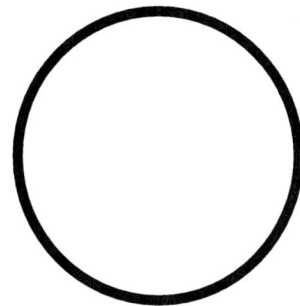

Following Directions and Aural Reasoning Bright Kids NYC Inc ©

07. Many stars big and small.

Blue is my favorite one of them all.

Of the pictures that you see, which one is best for me?

08. I have four corners like a square.

In the baseball field, you can find me everywhere.

Of the pictures that you see, which one is me?

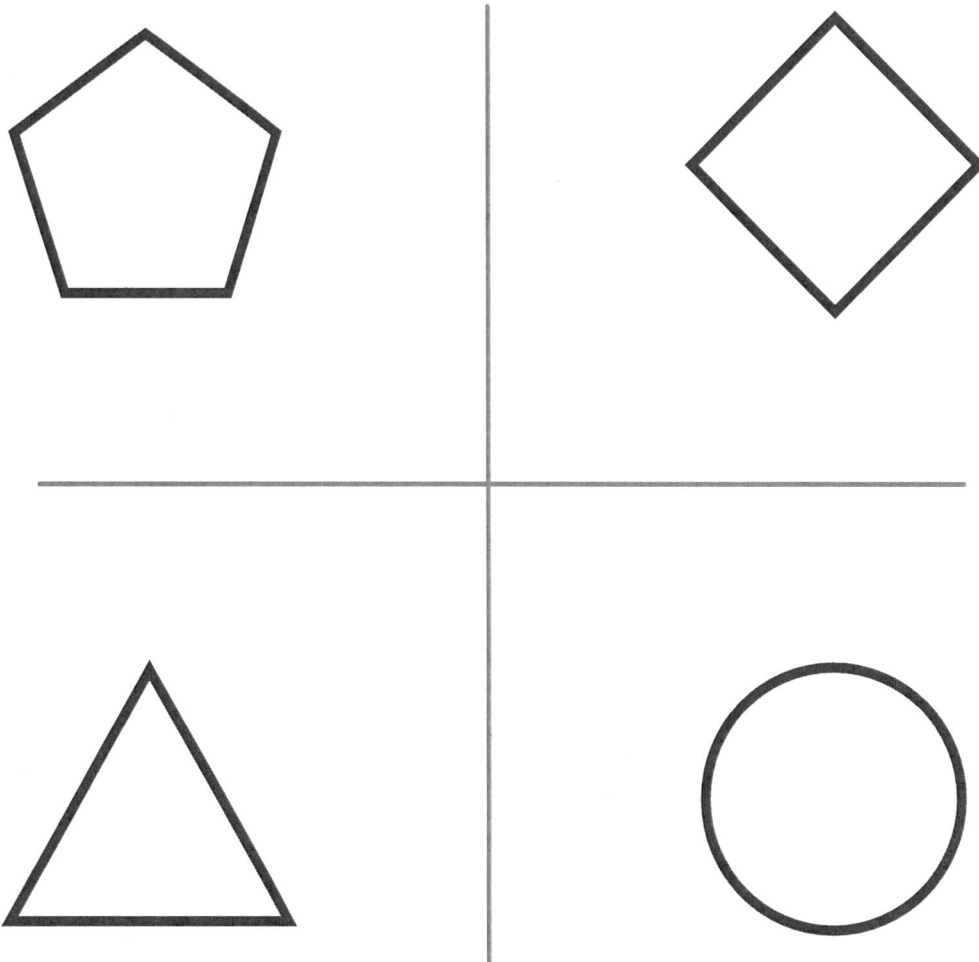

Following Directions and Aural Reasoning Bright Kids NYC Inc ©

09. Yellow and red, but we are a few,

with many sides and this is your last clue.

Of the groups that you see, which one is me?

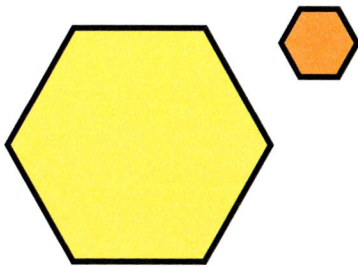

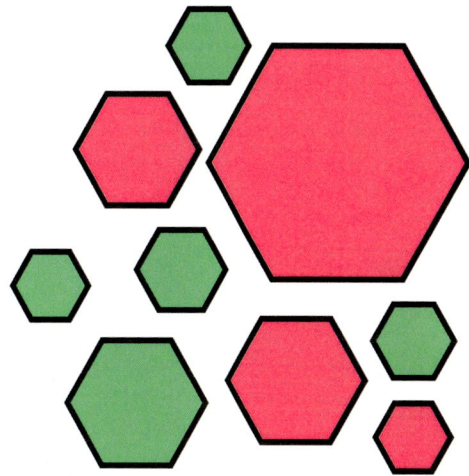

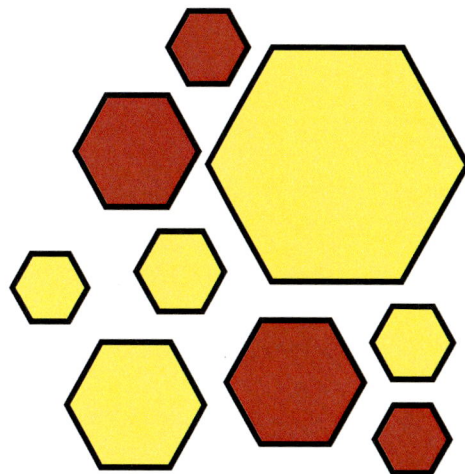

10. I am bigger then the rest.

Four sides make me the best.

Of the pictures that you see, which one is me?

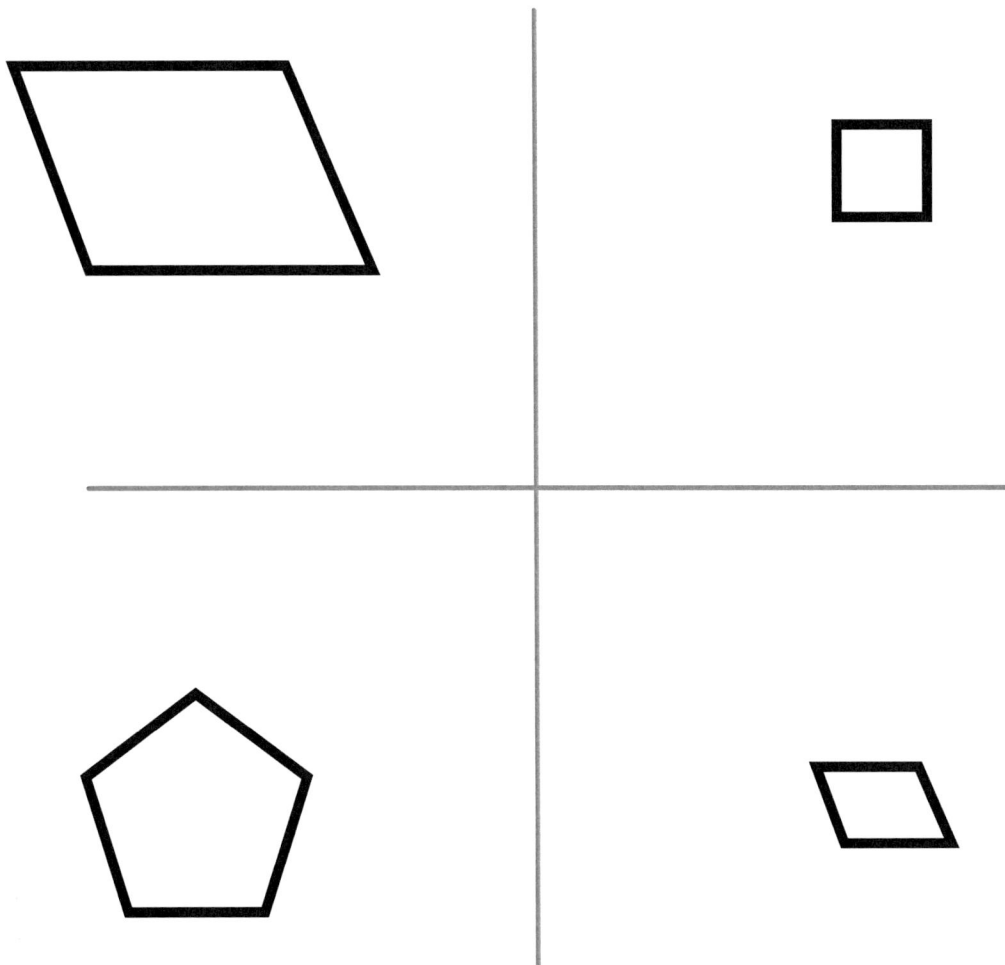

11. We get bigger as we go.

Look at the three of us as we grow.

Of the groups that you see, which one is me?

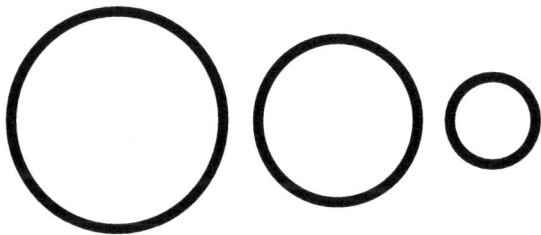

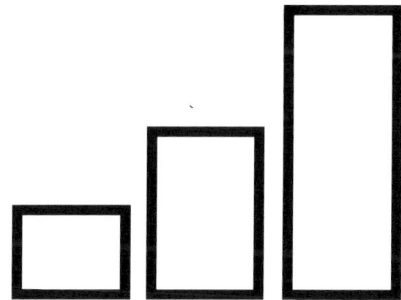

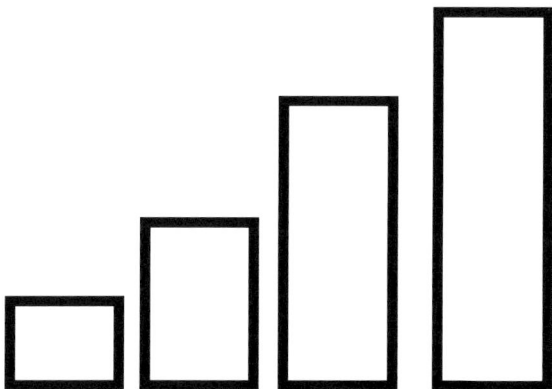

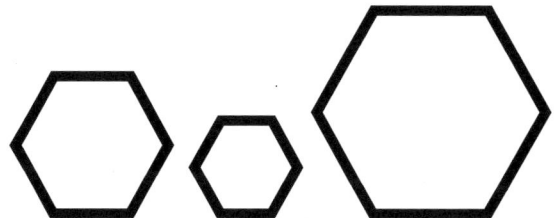

12. I love to camp.

I started a fire and lit a lamp.

Of the pictures that you see, which one is me?

13. **In a house like me, you may have found**

that it's unusual to see windows so round.

Of the pictures you see, which one is me?

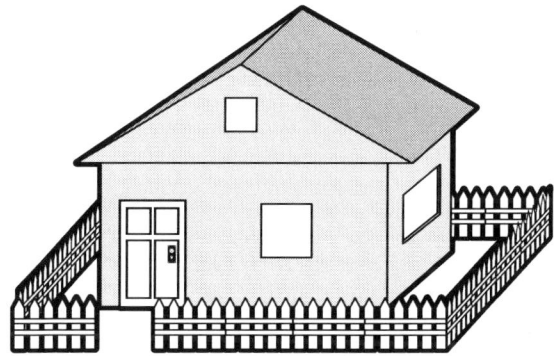

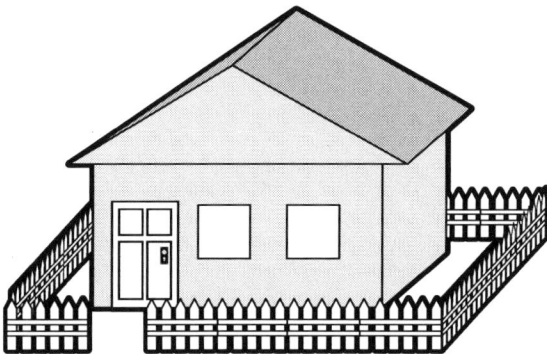

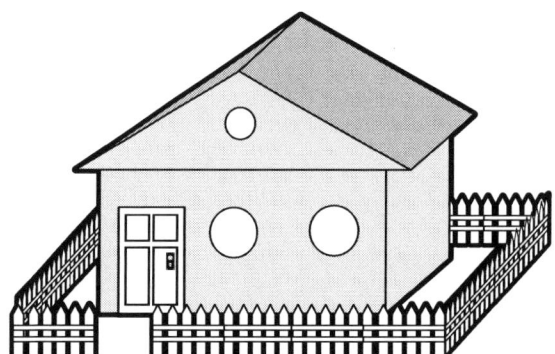

14. Jack drank some juice,

Jill drank some more,

Joe drank until there was no more.

If I am Joe's cup, of the pictures that you see, which one is me?

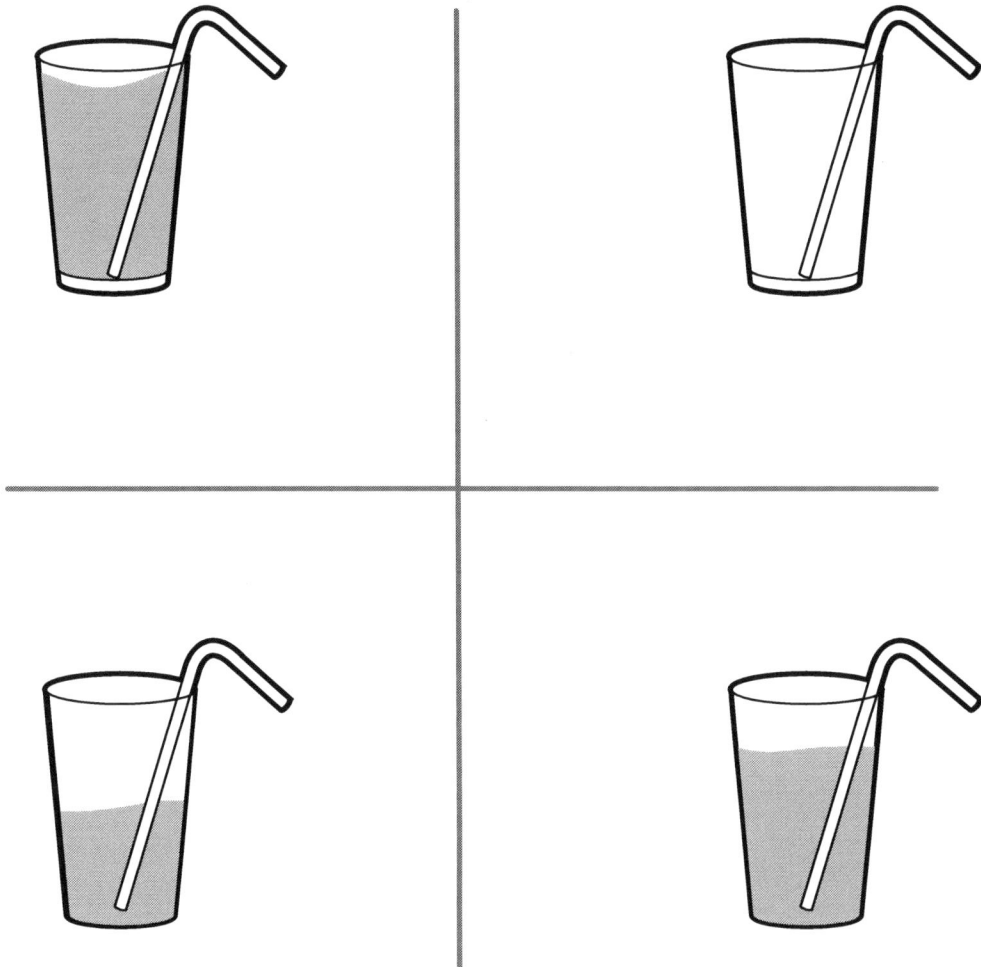

15. I have a bird and a bear,

together near a chair.

Of the pictures you see, which one is me?

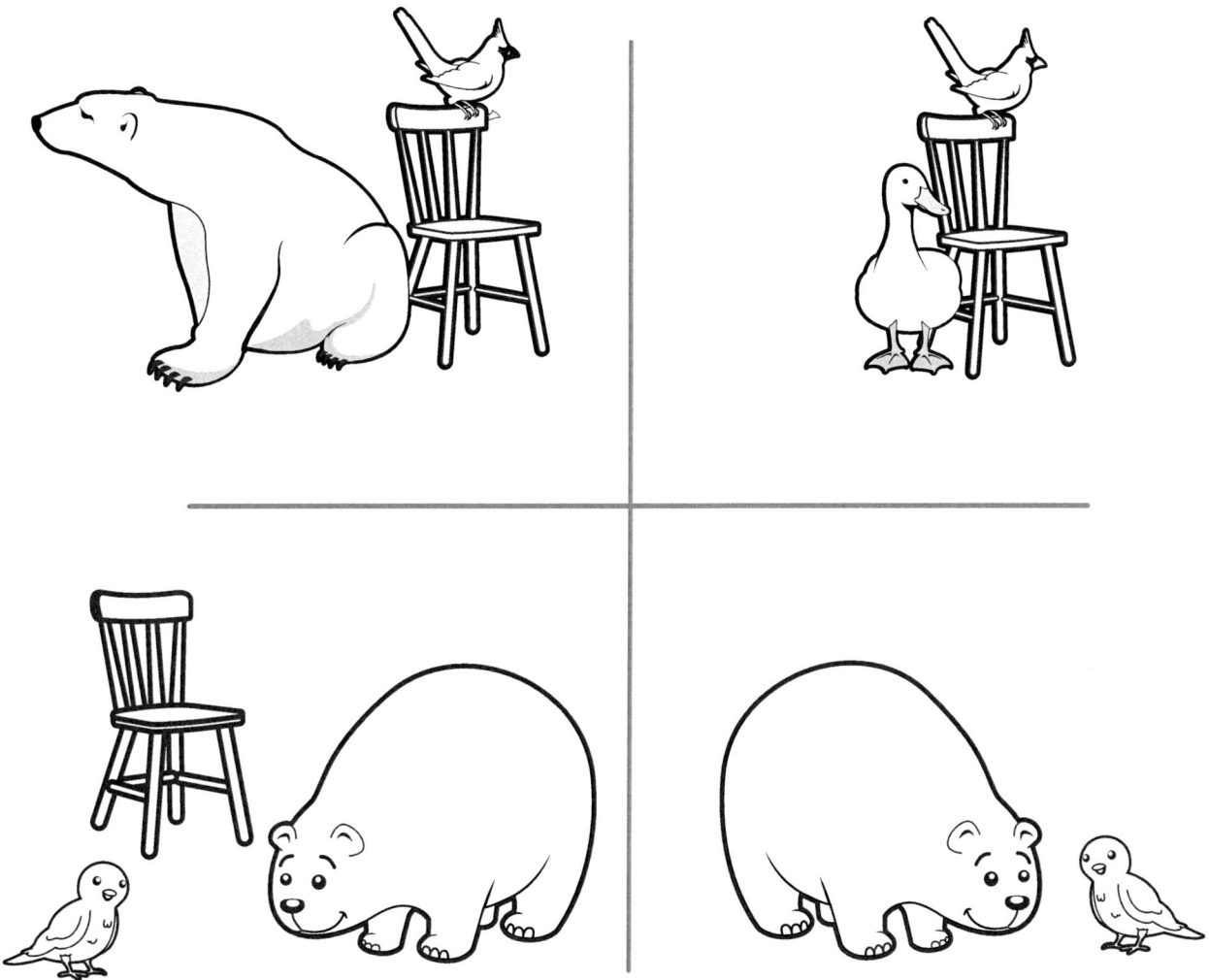

16. I have a blue baseball bat,

but I am not wearing a yellow hat.

Of the pictures you see, which one is me?

Following Directions and Aural Reasoning Bright Kids NYC Inc ©

17. **Baskets of apples you see,**

The one I like has less than three.

Of the pictures you see, which basket is for me?

18. I'm quite a bit different from these other three.

    See how they are alike, then you will find me.

    Of the pictures that you see, which one is me?

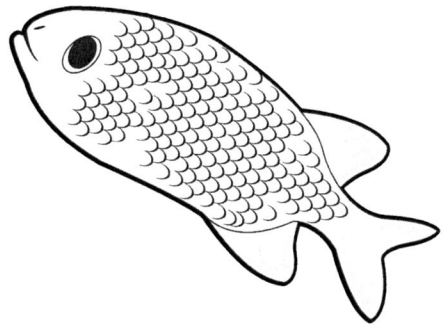

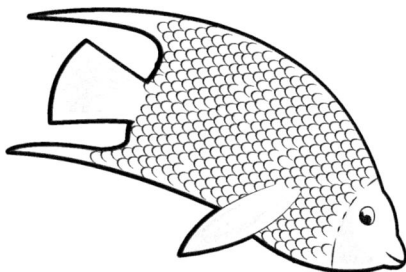

- -

19. I love pumpkins in the fall.

Mine is the scariest of them all.

Of the pictures you see, which pumpkin is for me?

20. **The musical instrument I like to play,**

   has no strings or keys in any way.

   Of the pictures you see, which instrument is for me?

21. **My house is green and the garage is blue.**

I have a car that's old and a car that's new.

Of the pictures that you see, which one is me?

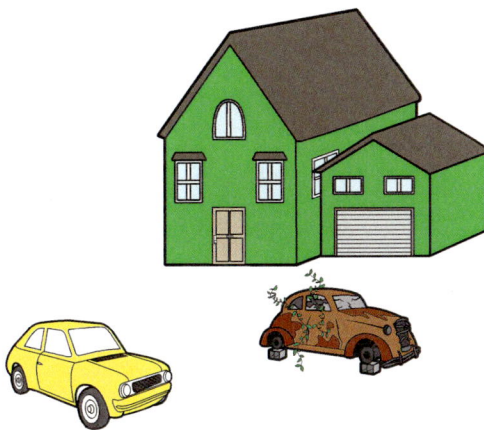

22. In the air I'm usually found,

especially since I don't run fast on the ground.

Of the pictures that you see, which one is me?

Following Directions and Aural Reasoning Bright Kids NYC Inc ©

23. **Black and white, behind the tree,**

when I get scared, it gets smelly.

Of the pictures that you see, which one is me?

24. A green frog ate a black ant.

A spotted snake ate the green frog,

A tiger ate the spotted snake, black ant, and green frog.

Of the pictures that you see, who is left in this story?

25. **May entered a pizza eating contest.**

She ate half of a pizza and then left the rest.

In front of her seat, which pizza did May eat?

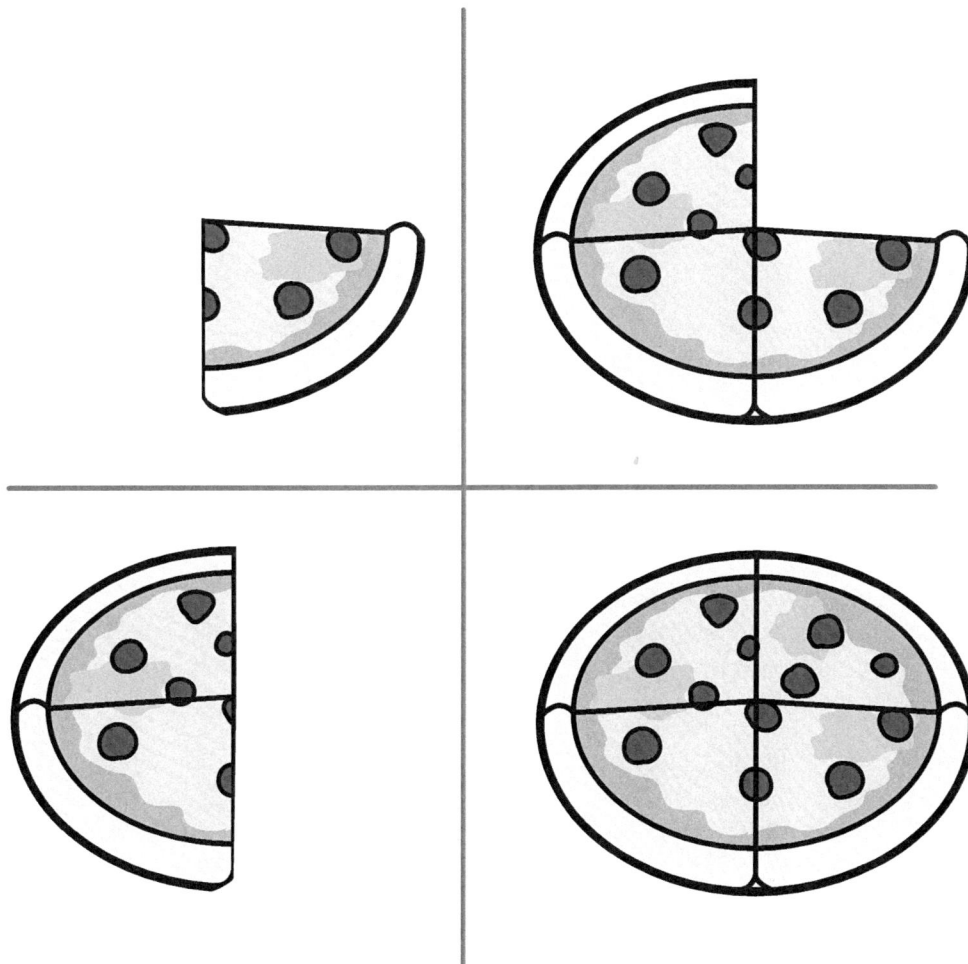

28. I am a boy who is short,

whose wearing a yellow hat and a blue coat.

Of the pictures you see, which one is me?

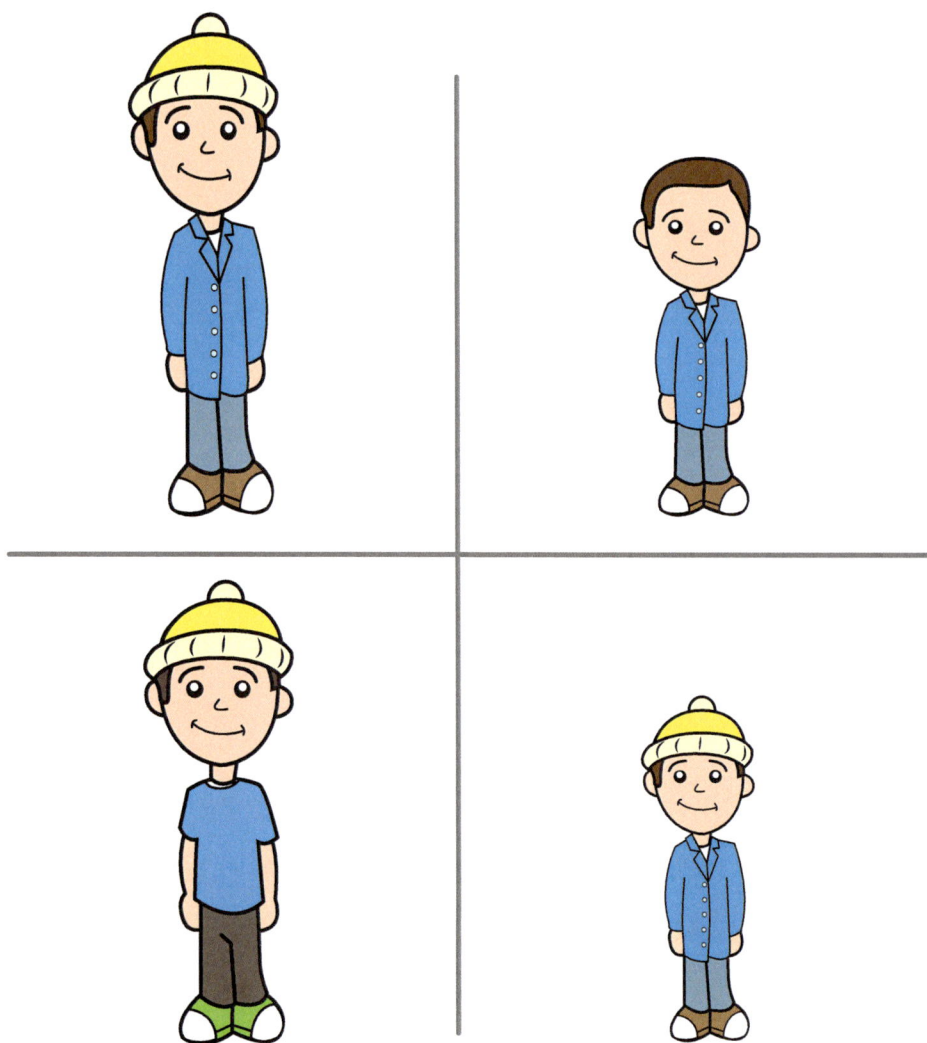

Following Directions and Aural Reasoning   Bright Kids NYC Inc ©

27. I have blocks, red and blue.

Making a tower with a few.

Of the pictures you see, which one is me?

28. I am Kai's brother Finn.

     My hair is red and I am thin.

     Of the pictures you see, which one is me?

29. **Annie is wearing a red hat,**

standing between a black and a gray cat.

Of the pictures you see, which one is Annie?

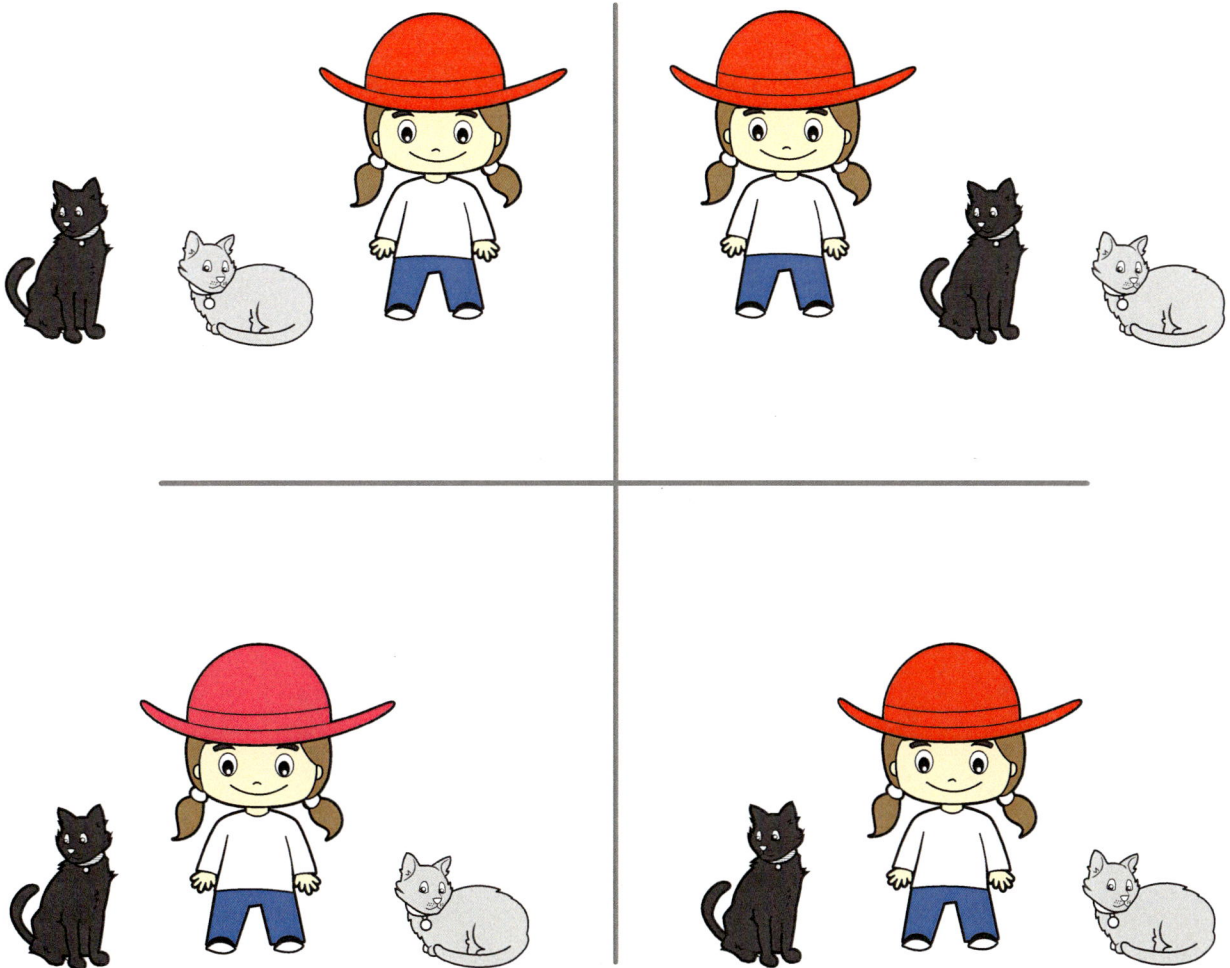

30. I am a red-eyed green frog,

sitting in between two logs.

Of the pictures you see, which one is me?

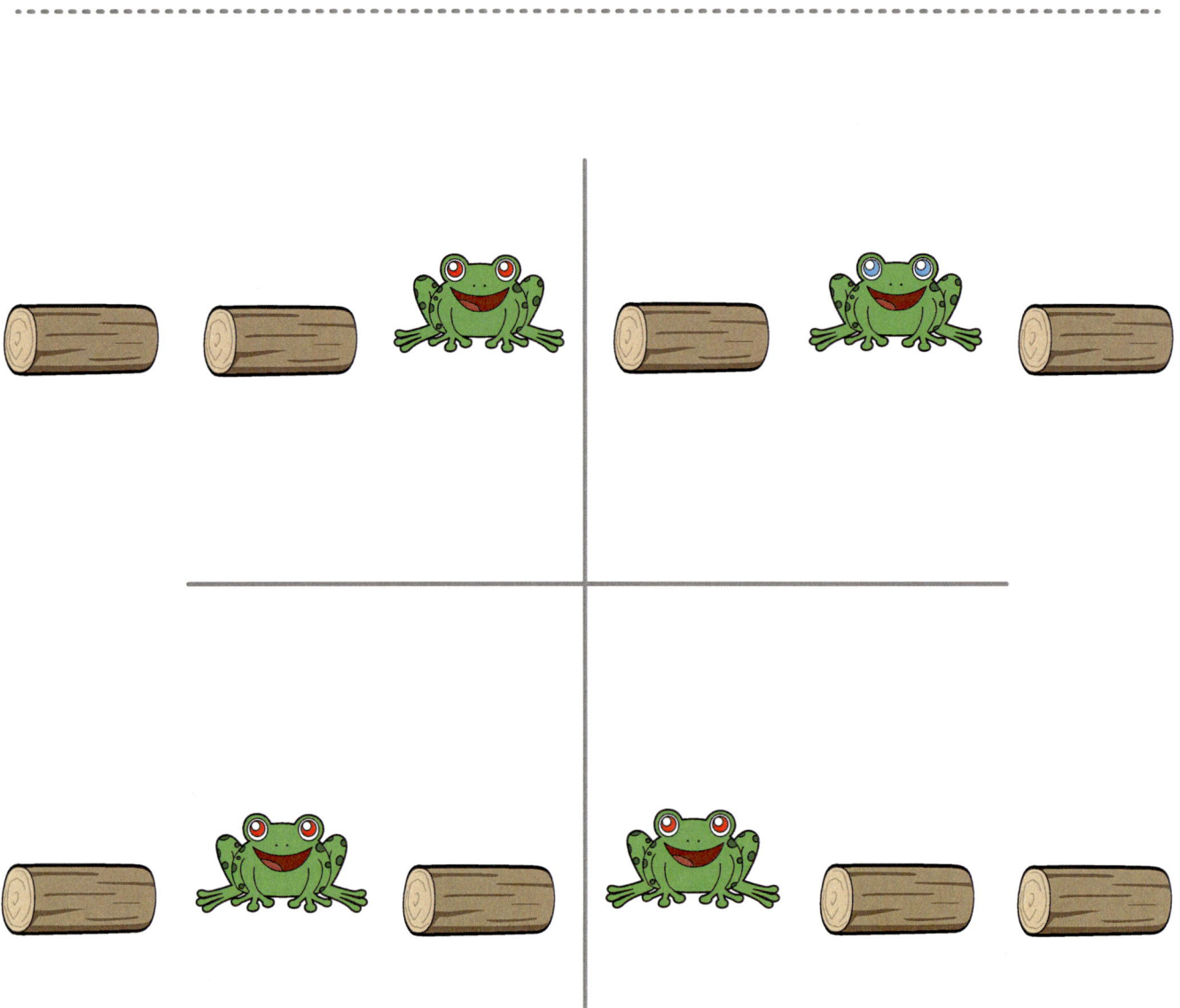

Chapter Three

Aural Directions

01.   Color the snowmen's scarves blue.

02.   Color the snowmen's hats purple.

03.   Color the snowmen's noses orange.

04.   Color the snowmen's arms brown.

05.   Draw three green buttons on the snowman.

06.   Draw a smile on the snowman.

07.   Draw two black eyes on the snowman.

01. Color the star-shaped balloon yellow.

02. Color the circular-shaped balloon orange.

03. Draw three blue stripes on the cylinder-shaped balloon.

04. Draw one red circle on the square-shaped balloon.

05. Draw three green triangles on the diamond-shaped balloon.

06. Draw a purple triangle-shaped balloon.

07. Draw a string on the star-shaped balloon.

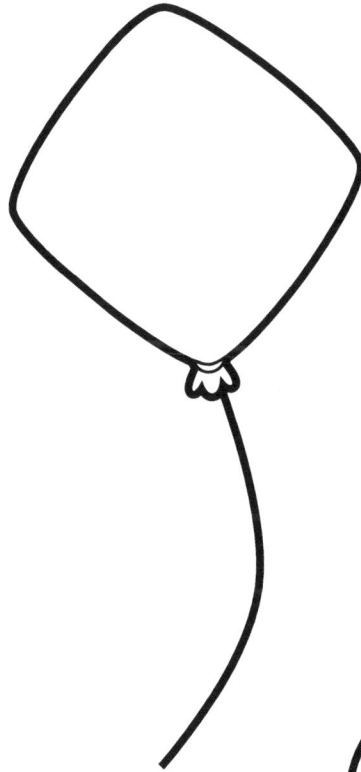

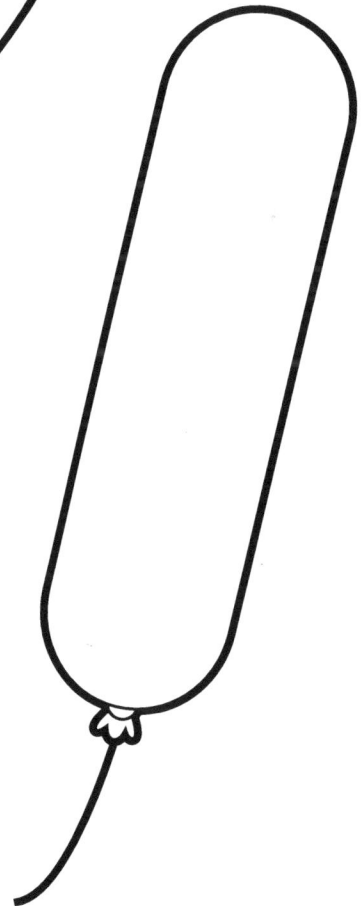

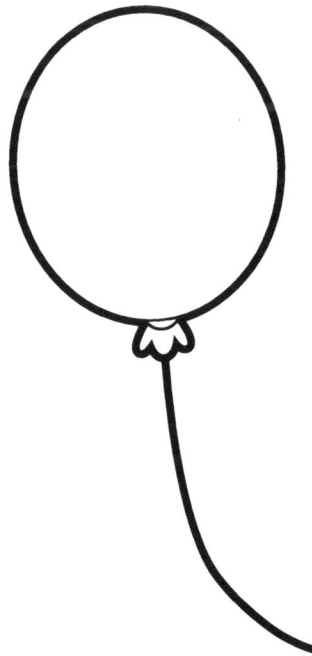

01. Color the turtle's skin green.

02. Color the butterfly blue.

03. Color the turtle's shell brown.

04. Color the petals pink.

05. Draw a yellow sun in the sky.

06. Draw another leaf on the flower.

07. Color the turtle's tongue red.

01. Draw an arrow pointing to the bird that is in a nest.

02. Two birds are flying above their nest. Color their nest brown.

03. Color the bird that is behind the nest blue.

04. Color the beak of the bird standing on a branch red and color its body yellow.

05. Color all of the nest eggs green except for one.

06. Circle the bird that is in a cage.

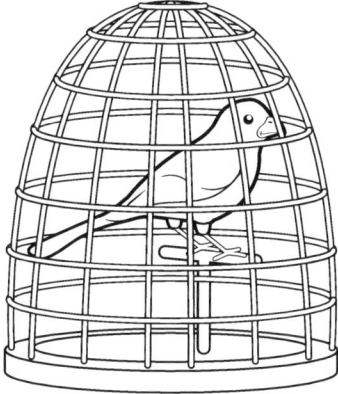

01. Put one line under the box with a hole in it.

02. Circle the closed rectangular box.

03. Color the turtle in the box. Color its shell red and its head brown.

04. Put an "X" on the circular box.

05. Circle the box that is open and empty.

06. Color the box that is full yellow.

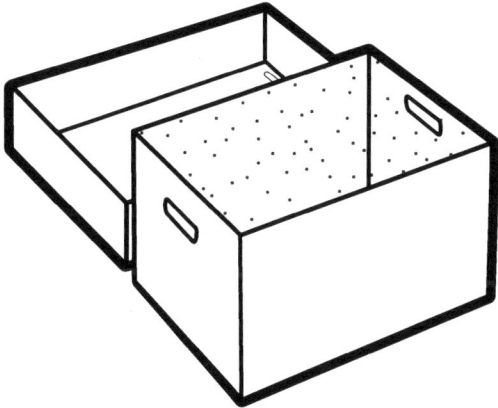

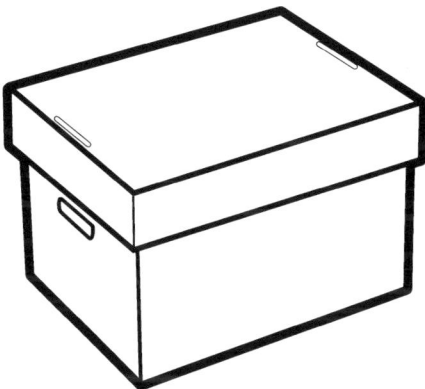

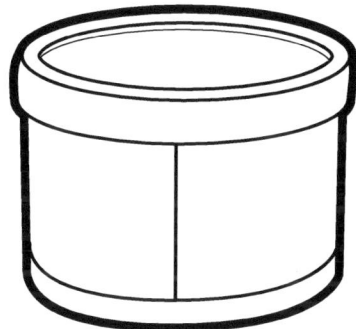

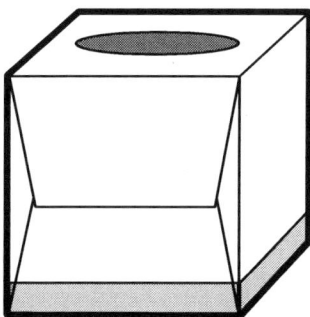

01. Draw a square around the things that are arranged in a square.

02. Put an "X" on three different things that are in a row.

03. Put a line under the things that are alike and in a row.

04. Color in the pictures that show animals.

05. Color all of the objects arranged in a circle a different color.

06. Draw two lines under the pictures that show things that are alike.

01. Color the shirt of the boy standing in between two girls red.

02. Draw two circles around the small boy who is standing next to a big house.

03. Color the pants on the girl who is standing next to a dollhouse blue.

04. Circle the girls who have a boy standing in between them.

05. Draw two lines under the short boy who is standing next to a tall girl.

06. Color the garage of the big house red and color the house yellow.

01. Find the rabbit that is on top of a carrot and color the rabbit yellow.

02. Color the carrot that is under the rabbit orange.

03. Find the rabbit in front of a carrot and draw a circle around the carrot.

04. Draw an "X" on the backward facing rabbit.

05. Color the rabbit that is facing forward green.

06. Circle the rabbit that has a pile of carrots.

01. Circle something you can rest on.

02. Put two lines on top of the object that cleans clothing.

03. Draw two arrows that point to the object that keeps food cold.

04. Circle the object that cleans the floor.

05. Color the object that holds clothes blue.

06. Draw one line above and below the object that cooks food.

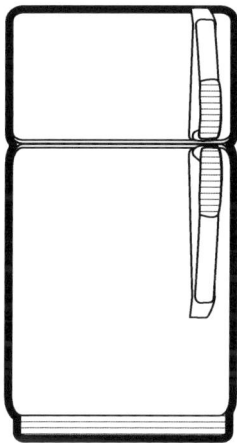

01. Color the butterfly with stripes blue.

02. Color the butterfly with the longest wings orange.

03. Color the smallest butterfly green.

04. Color the butterfly in the upper left-hand corner yellow.

05. Color the butterfly with dots purple.

06. Color the butterfly with a flower in its mouth blue.

07. Color the butterfly on the flower red.

01. Draw a circle in the second star and an "x" in the first one.

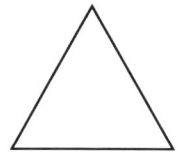

02. Draw a line connecting from the top of the first circle to the top of the fourth circle. Write a capital "M" in the second circle.

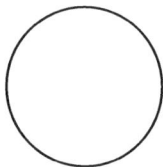

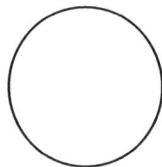

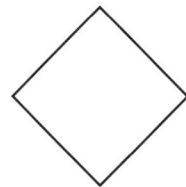

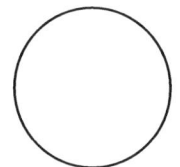

03. Underline the animal that crawls. Draw a square around the fourth animal.

04. Draw a square around the first two numbers. Draw a cross on the numbers that are greater than 6.

8   3   5   10

05. Color in the things that grow green. Draw two circles around the things that need water.

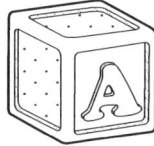

06. Draw a line from the second animal to the third animal. Underline the animal that is facing forward.

07. Draw a zigzag line over the unsharpened pencil. Draw three circles around the pencil that's been used the most.

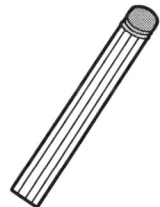

08. Draw two lines under the bird that is flying. Draw an "X" over the bird that is facing left.

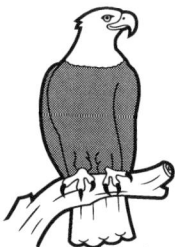

09. Draw two lines under the animals that are in pairs. Draw a squiggly line on top of the animals in groups of three.

10. If there are three numbers and one is greater than eight, draw a square in the circle.

1 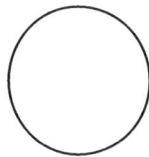 9 7

11. If there is a number greater than six, color the ship red. If there is a number less than six, color the ship blue.

3 5 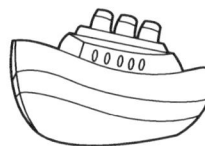 6

12. Circle the second largest number. If this number is greater than seven, color the castle yellow. If this number is less than seven, color the castle green.

 4 6 8

Chapter Four

Treasure Maps

AHOY MATEY!

01. Circle one large animal with claws and three small animals that also have claws.

02. Draw a square around the object that the pirate could use to better see the ship in the distance.

03. Color the parrot green.

04. Draw a rectangle around the animal that has eight legs.

05. Draw an "X" through the object that can be used to steer ship.

Following Directions and Aural Reasoning

Bright Kids NYC Inc ©

AHOY MATEY!

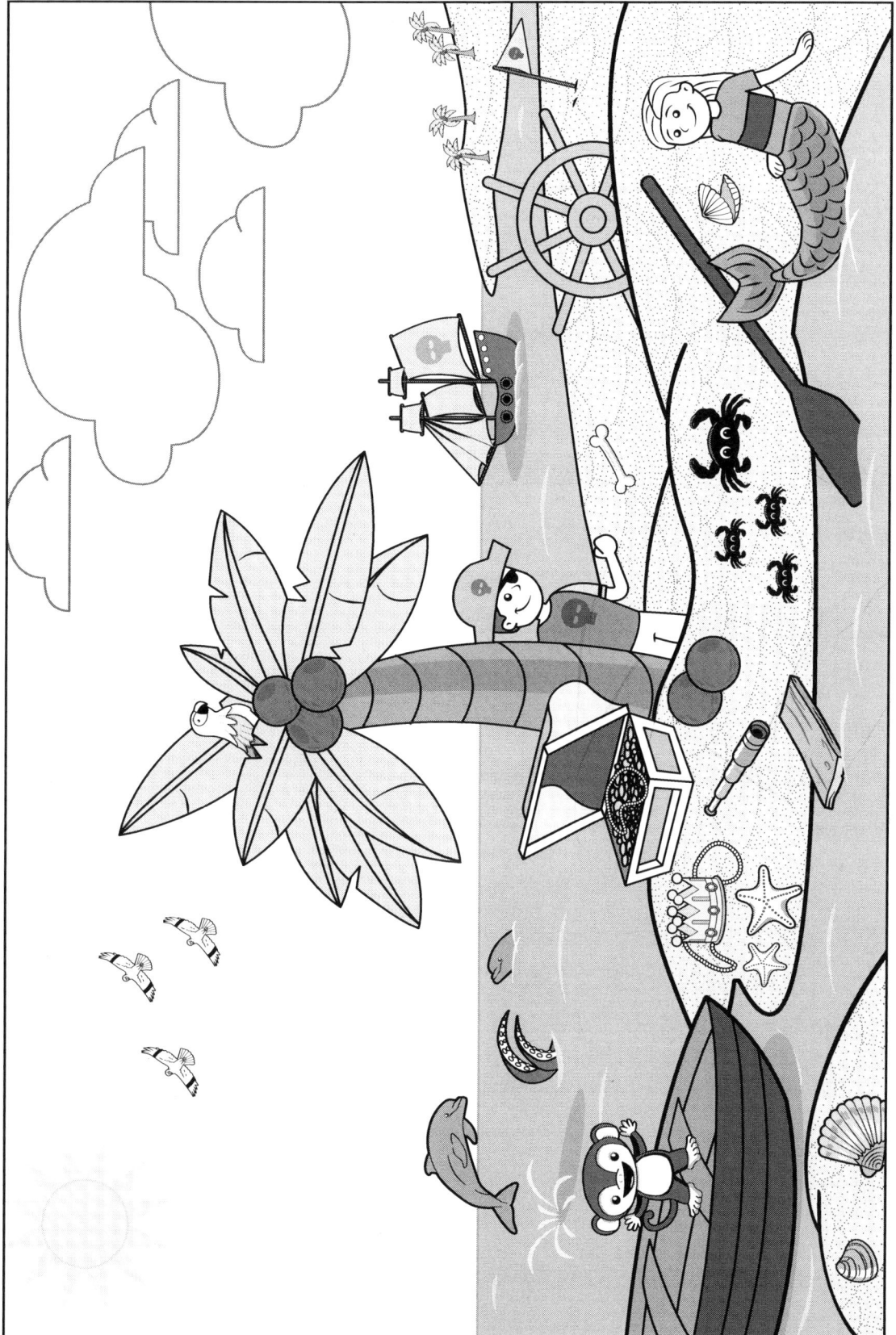

ARCADE MANIA

01. Draw circles around the people that have stripes on their shirts.

02. Timmy can't drink his can of soda anymore. Draw an arrow pointing to what happened to Timmy's can of soda.

03. Draw a square around the poster that shows three people competing in a race.

04. Suzanne saw an object on the floor that is very light and can fly through the air. Draw a rectangle around this object.

05. Find the person who is wearing a hat and color his shirt red.

Following Directions and Aural Reasoning

Bright Kids NYC Inc ©

Arcade Mania

RUNNING

Arcade

BARN YARN

01. Draw a square around an animal that a person typically rides on.

02. Color all of the birds, except for the chicken, in the picture blue.

03. Circle the machine that needs wind in order to work properly.

04. Draw an "X" underneath the sleeping animal.

05. Draw a rectangle around the animal that is very fluffy.

Following Directions and Aural Reasoning

Bright Kids NYC Inc ©

BARN YARN

OUT OF THIS WORLD

01. Color the alien's uniform orange.

02. Color the oceans of the Earth blue.

03. Circle all of the satellites in the picture.

04. Draw a square around the planets that are not Earth.

05. Draw an "X" through all of the comets in the picture.

Following Directions and Aural Reasoning Bright Kids NYC Inc ©

OUT OF THIS WORLD

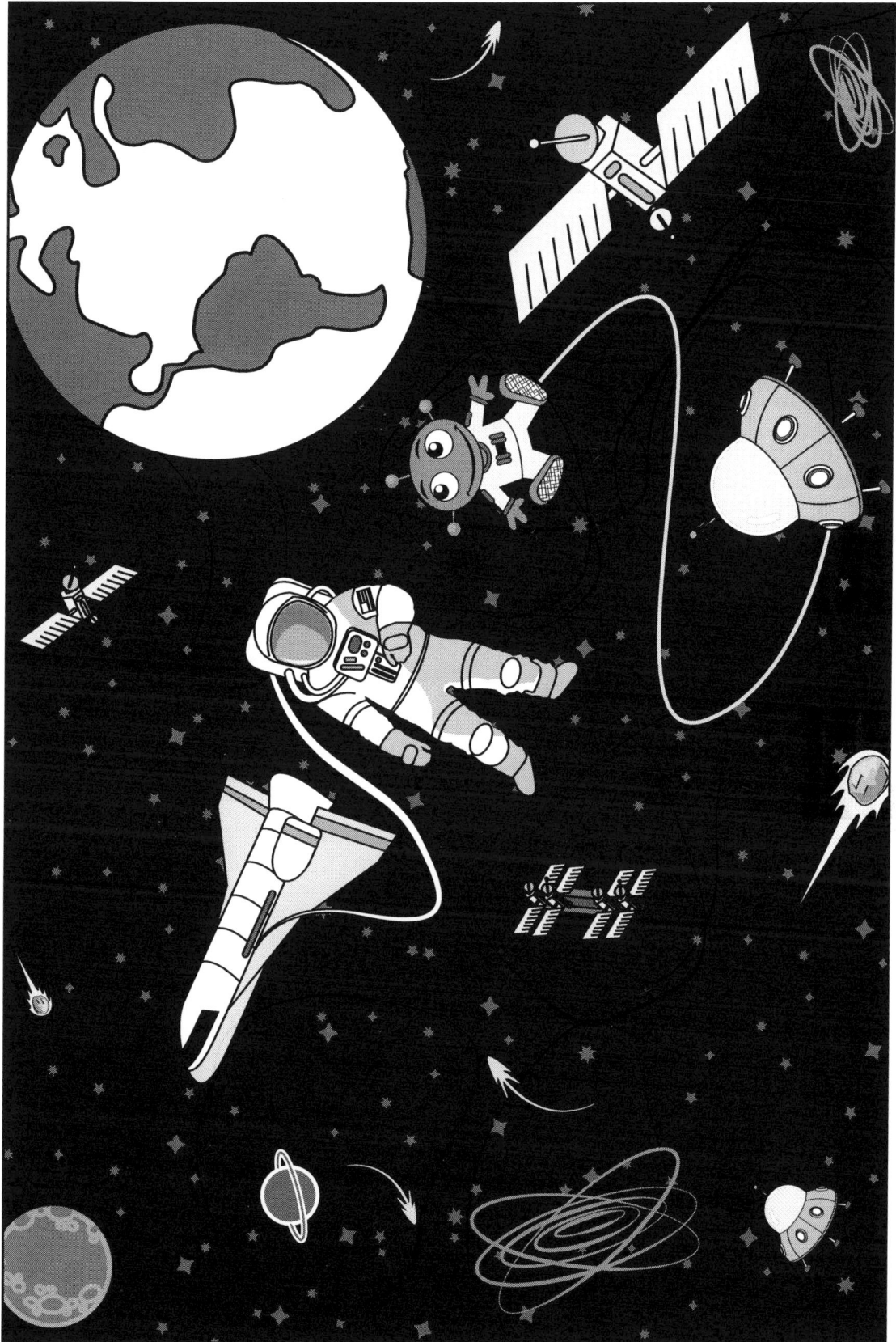

FUN IN THE SUN

01. Draw a square around the two people who are trying to fly something with a string.

02. Circle the lizard.

03. Draw a rectangle around the object that is made of sand.

04. Put an "X" under two objects that can float in water.

05. Draw a line under all of the objects that are capable of flying.

FUN IN THE SUN

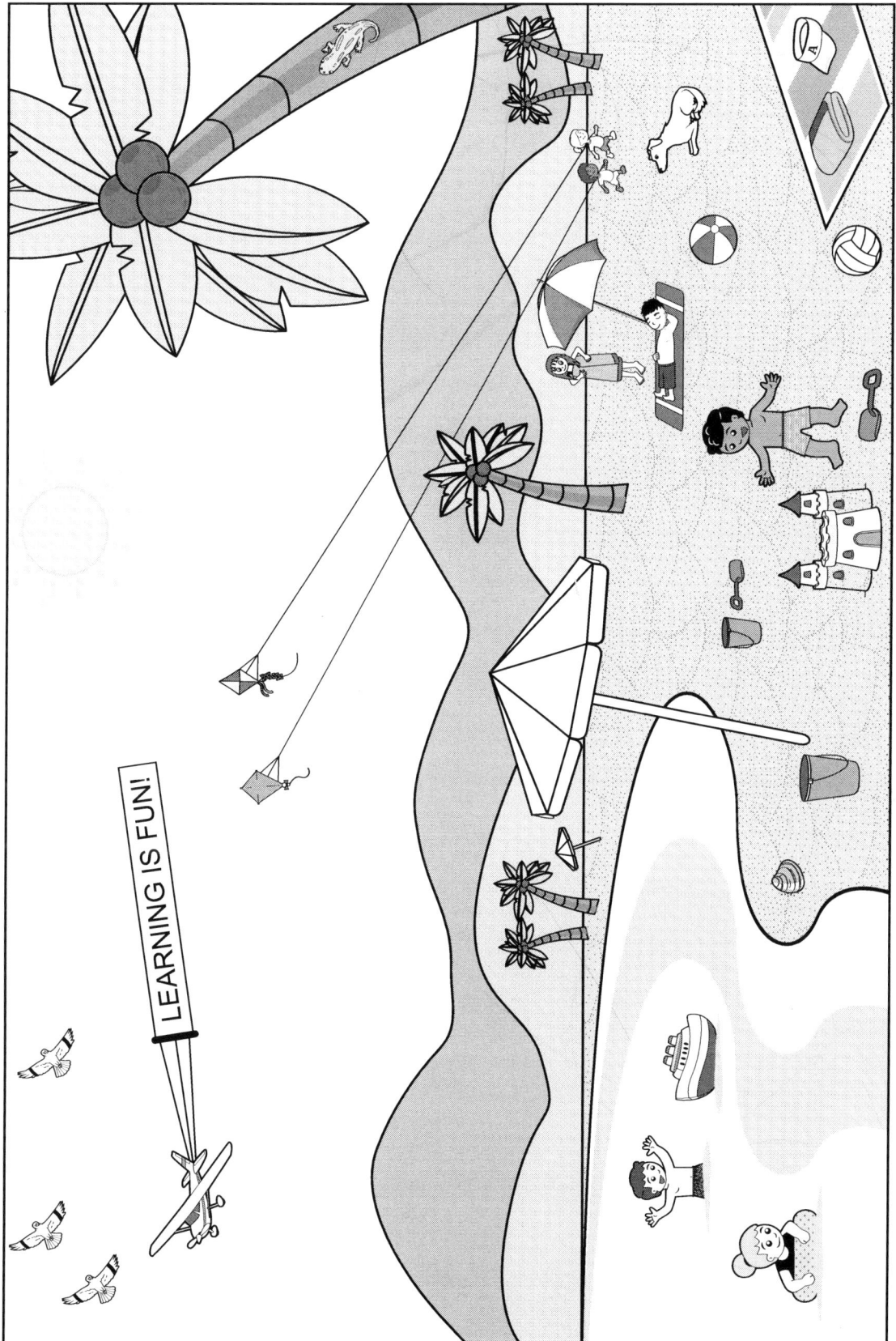

LEARNING IS FUN!

Back To School

01. Draw a rectangle around the poster of an animal that hops.

02. Color the shirts of all the boys in the picture blue.

03. If it was raining outside, circle the objects that some of the students may have brought to class.

04. Jerry just gave Mr. London a present. Draw a square around the present that Jerry just put on Mr. London's desk.

05. Alex left something you can use to measure the size of items with on his chair. Draw a line underneath this item.

Following Directions and Aural Reasoning

Bright Kids NYC Inc ©

BACK TO SCHOOL

Aa Bb Cc Dd Ee Ff Gg Hh Ii Jj Kk Ll Mm Nn Oo Pp Qq Rr Ss

Mr. LONDON'S CLASSROOM

Following Directions and Aural Reasoning Bright Kids NYC Inc ©

Chapter Five

Following Directions

03. Look at the four pictures.

Level 1: Point to the picture with one mouse.
Level 2: Point to the picture with a cat in front of the tree.
Level 3: Point to the picture that has two mice in front of the tree in between a dog and a pair of cats.

05. Look at the four pictures.

Level 1: Point to the picture that has two small dogs.
Level 2: Point to the picture where there is a small dog in between a big dog and a polar bear.
Level 3: Polar bears are zaps, small dogs are tiks and big dogs are keps. Point to the picture that shows this: Keps-tiks-zaps-zaps.

Following Directions and Aural Reasoning

Bright Kids NYC Inc ©

01. Look at the four pictures.

Level 1: Point to the picture without a tree.
Level 2: Point to the pair of squirrels on top of a table.
Level 3: Point to the picture that has a squirrel on top of the table and a squirrel below the table in between two chairs.

1

2

3

4

02. Look at the four pictures.

Level 1: Point to the picture with two kites.

Level 2: Point to the picture where all of the kids, except for one, are eating ice cream.

Level 3: Point to the picture where two children are eating ice cream and standing in between a girl holding a kite and a boy holding a gift.

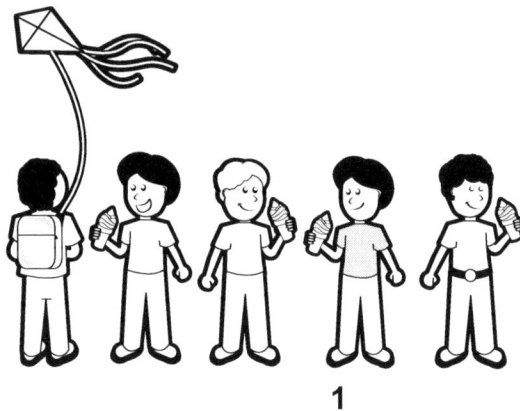

1

2

3

4

03. **Look at the four pictures.**

Level 1: Point to the picture with one mouse.
Level 2: Point to the picture that shows two cats sitting next to a tree.
Level 3: Point to the picture that shows a mouse sitting in between a dog and a cat.

1

2

3

4

04. Look at the four pictures.

Level 1: Point to the picture with a boy.

Level 2: Point to the picture where the girl is sitting in front of the computer.

Level 3: Point to the picture that shows a girl sitting in between a bookcase and a desk that has a computer on it.

05. **Look at the four pictures.**

Level 1: Point to the picture that has two small dogs.
Level 2: Point to the picture where there is a small dog in between a big dog and a polar bear.
Level 3: Polar bears are zaps, small dogs are tiks, and big dogs are keps.
Point to the picture that shows this: Keps-zaps-zaps-tiks.

1	2
3	4

06. Look at the four pictures.

Level 1: Point to the picture that has two circles.

Level 2: Point to the picture where there is a rectangle below a triangle that has a small triangle inside of it.

Level 3: Point the picture that has a small triangle inside of a large triangle with a circle below the two triangles.

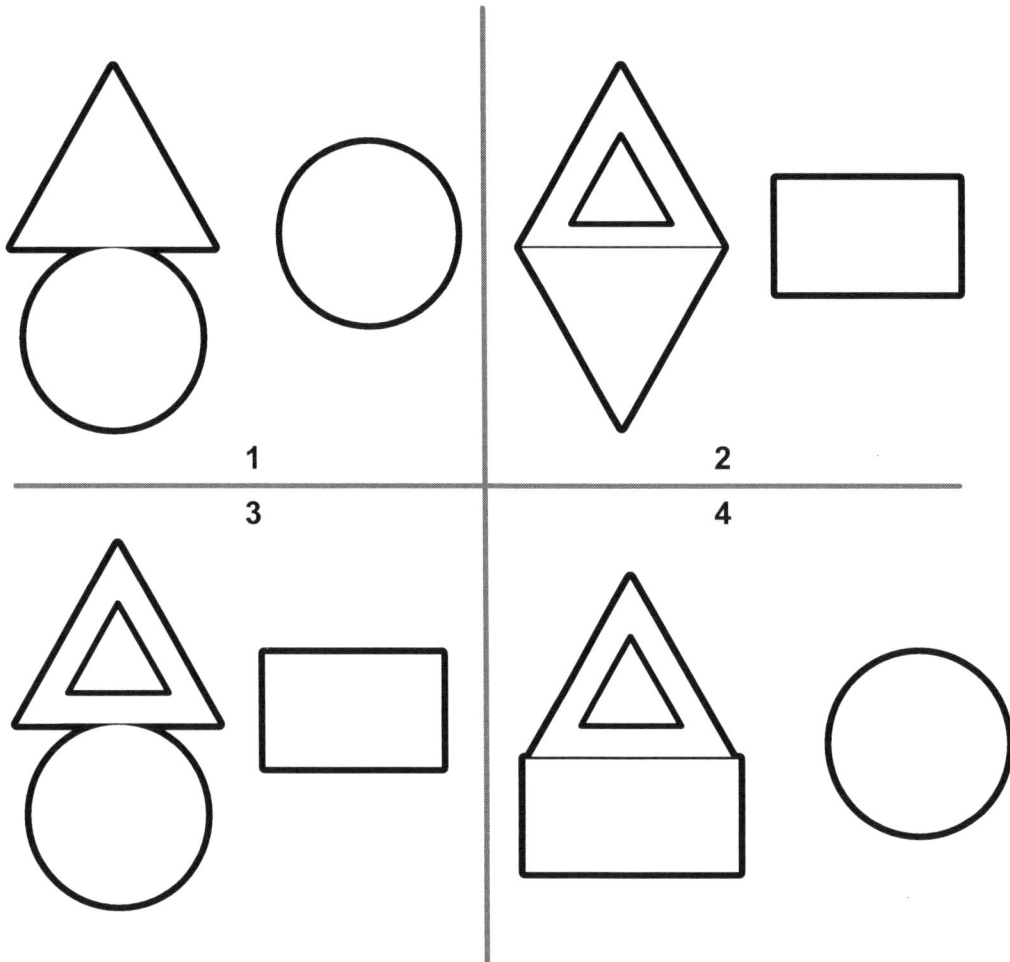

1

2

3

4

Following Directions and Aural Reasoning   Bright Kids NYC Inc ©

07. Look at the four pictures.

Level 1: Point to the picture that has a forward facing duck.
Level 2: Point to the picture where there is one white cat and one white rabbit.
Level 3: Point to the picture that has a backwards facing duck standing in between a black cat and a white rabbit.

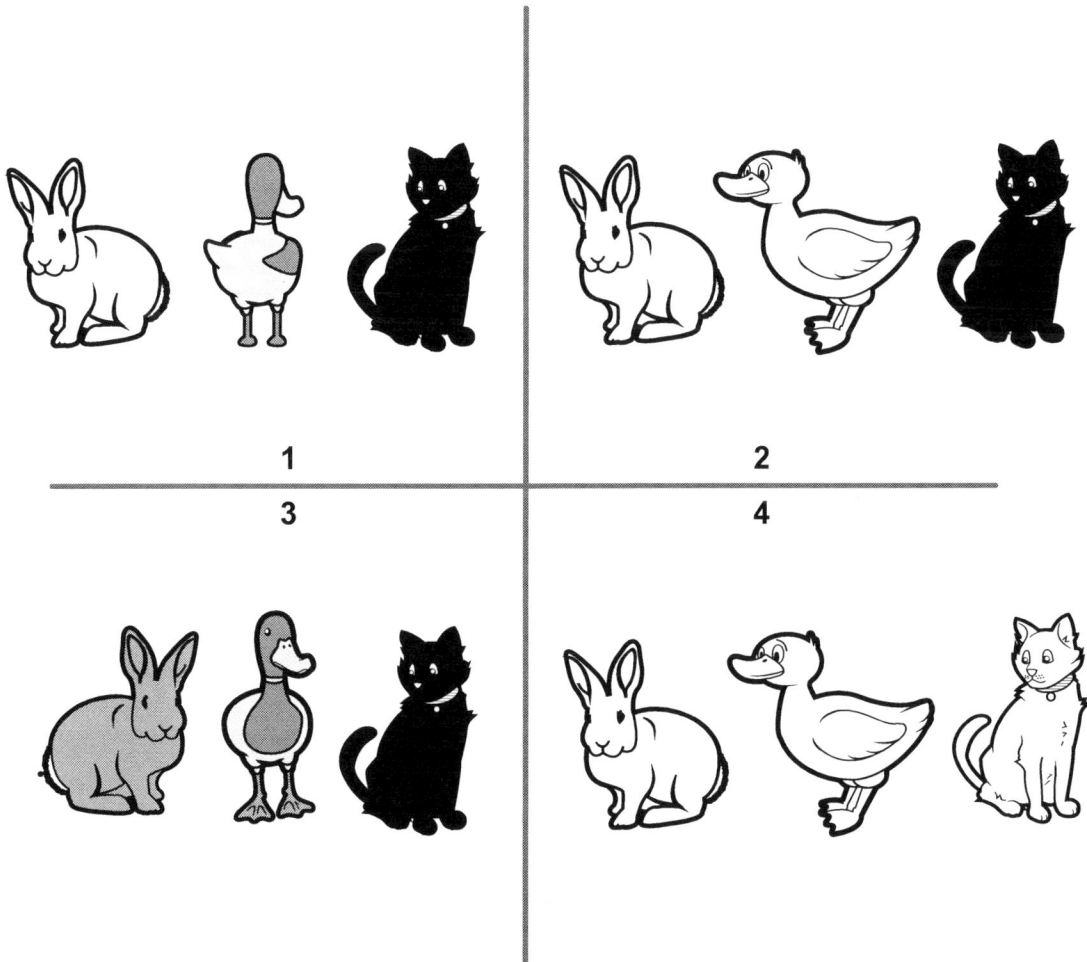

1

2

3

4

08. **Look at the four pictures.**

Level 1: **Point to the picture that only has white shapes.**
Level 2: **Point to the picture that has a white circle in between a black triangle and a black square.**
Level 3: **Circles are mits, squares are zots, and triangles are nuks. Point to the picture that shows this: nuks-mits-zots.**

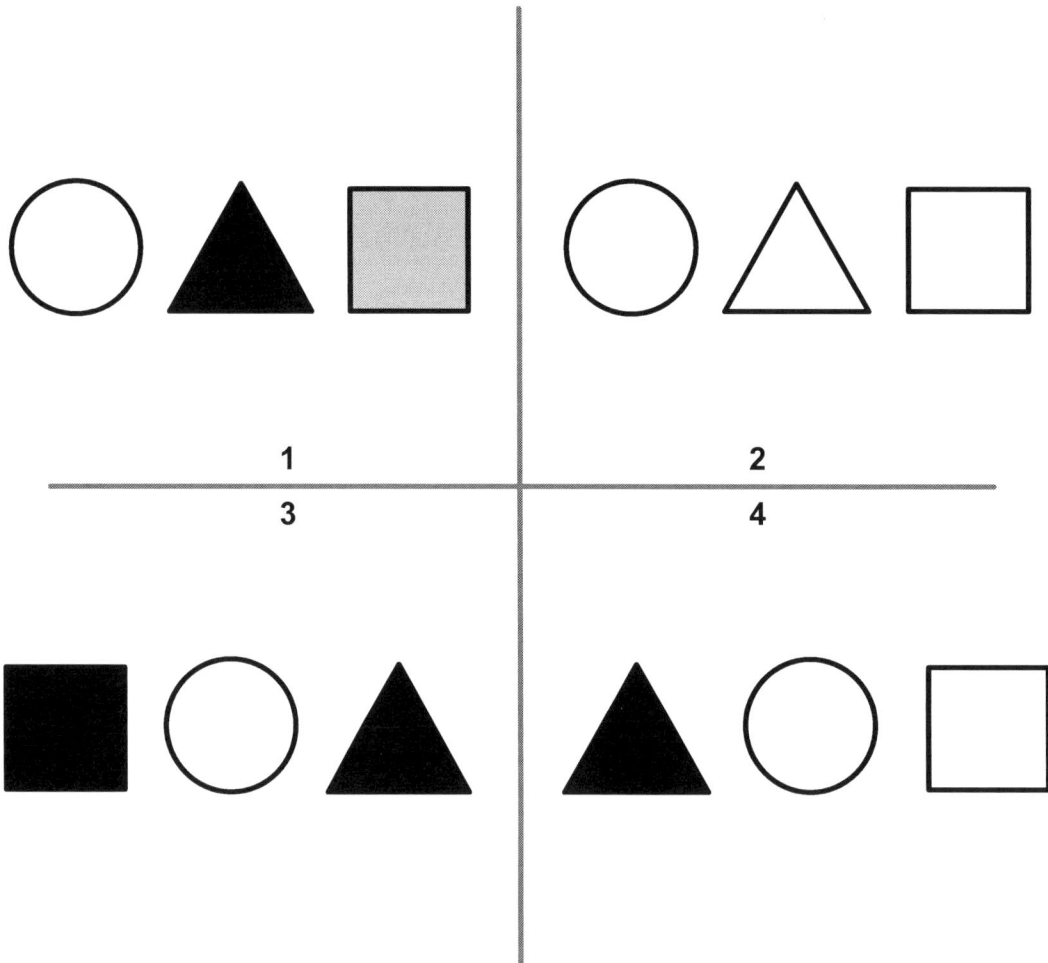

1

2

3

4

09. Look at the four pictures.

Level 1: Point to the picture that has two hearts.

Level 2: Point to the picture where there is black circle on top of the other shapes.

Level 3: Point the picture that has a pair of white triangles that are in between a white heart on top and a black circle that is below them.

10. **Look at the four pictures.**

Level 1: Point to the picture that only has two roses.
Level 2: Point to the picture that has that has no tulips.
Level 3: Point to the picture that has a vase with both tulips and roses, but but only has one sunflower.

1   2

3   4

11. Look at the four pictures.

Level 1: Point to the picture that only has a white heart and a white square.

Level 2: Point to the picture that has a black square inside of a white square.

Level 3: Point to the picture that shows a square to the left of a white heart with a small black heart inside of it.

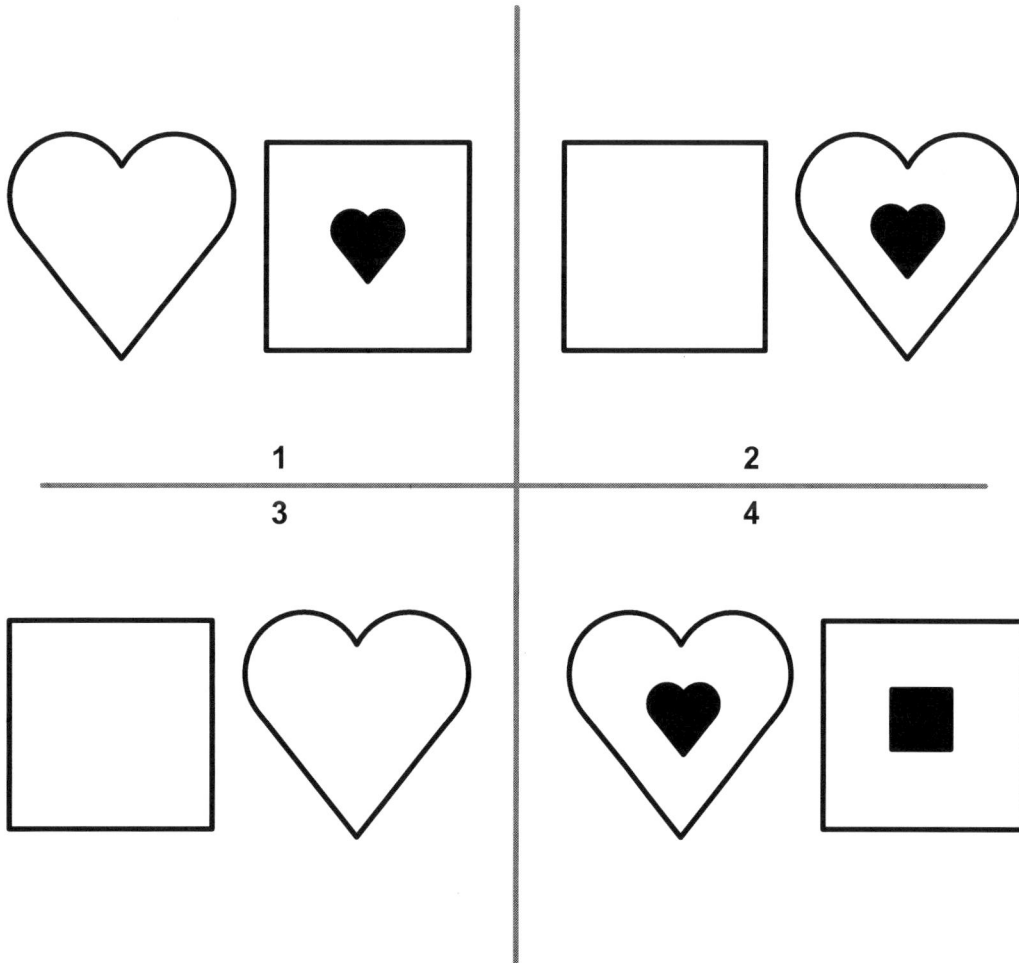

1   2

3   4

12. Look at the four pictures.

Level 1: Point to the picture that only shows one child.

Level 2: Point to the picture that shows two girls sitting next to a man and a woman.

Level 3: Point to the picture that shows a man with a hat sitting next to a woman who has a pair of kids sitting next to her.

1

2

3

4

Following Directions and Aural Reasoning Bright Kids NYC Inc ©

13. Look at the four pictures.

Level 1: Point to the picture that has two circles.

Level 2: Point to the picture that shows a black circle in between two white shapes.

Level 3: Point to the picture that shows three triangles stacked on top of each each other that are in between a black circle and a white square.

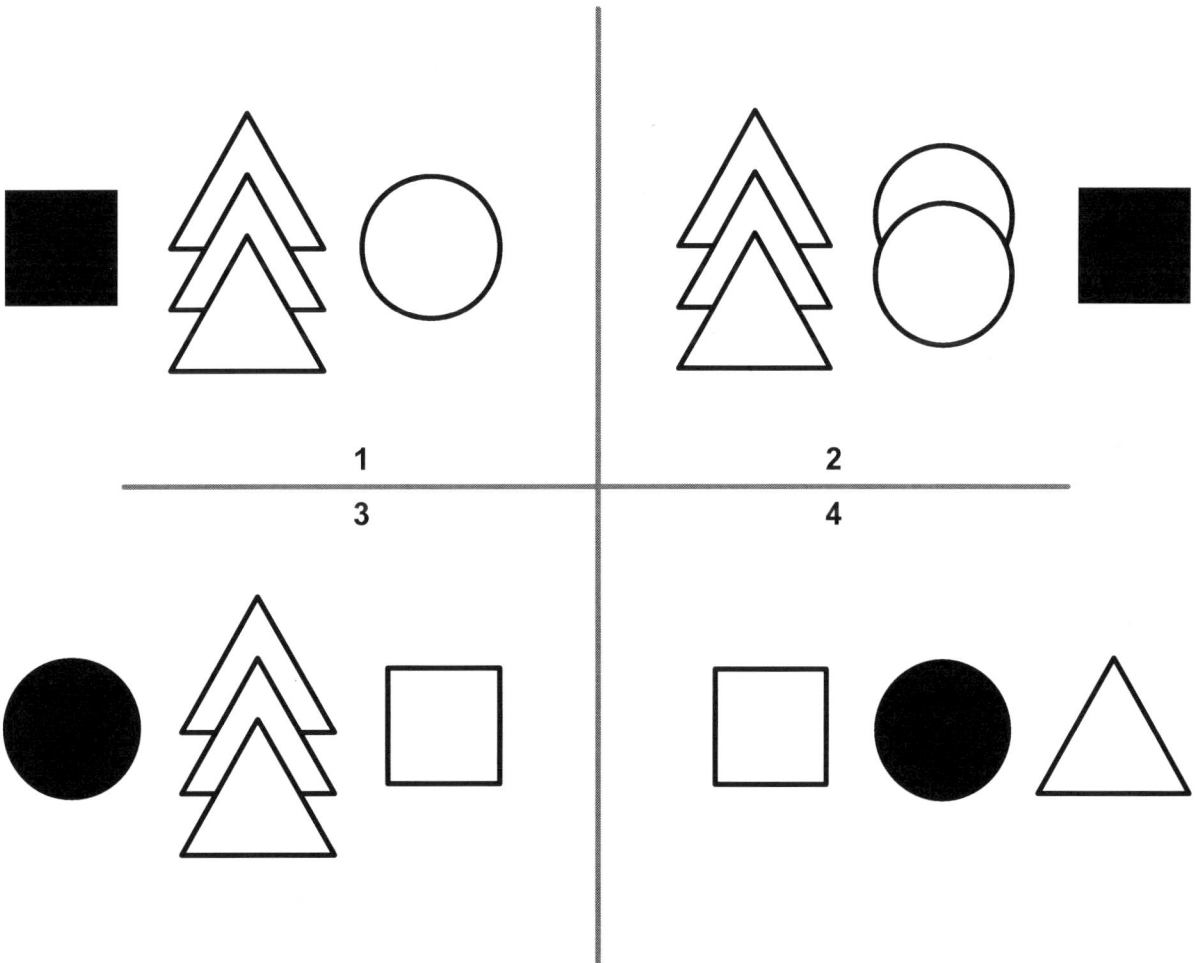

1

3

2

4

14. **Look at the chart with numbers, letters, and shapes in it.**

Level 1: Point to the number above the letter "F".

Level 2: Point to the number below a star that is next to a triangle.

Level 3: Point to the number below a triangle that is in between the letter "F" and the number "5".

★	2	★	△	4
2	○	5	1	F
A	★	△	B	○
△	6	○	8	★

15. Look at the four pictures.

Level 1: Point to the picture that does not have two triangles in it.

Level 2: Point to the picture that shows two white triangles on top of each other that are in between two white circles that have two smaller black circles inside of them.

Level 3: Point to the picture that shows two triangles on top of each other that are to the left of a white circle and a white circle with a black circle inside of it.

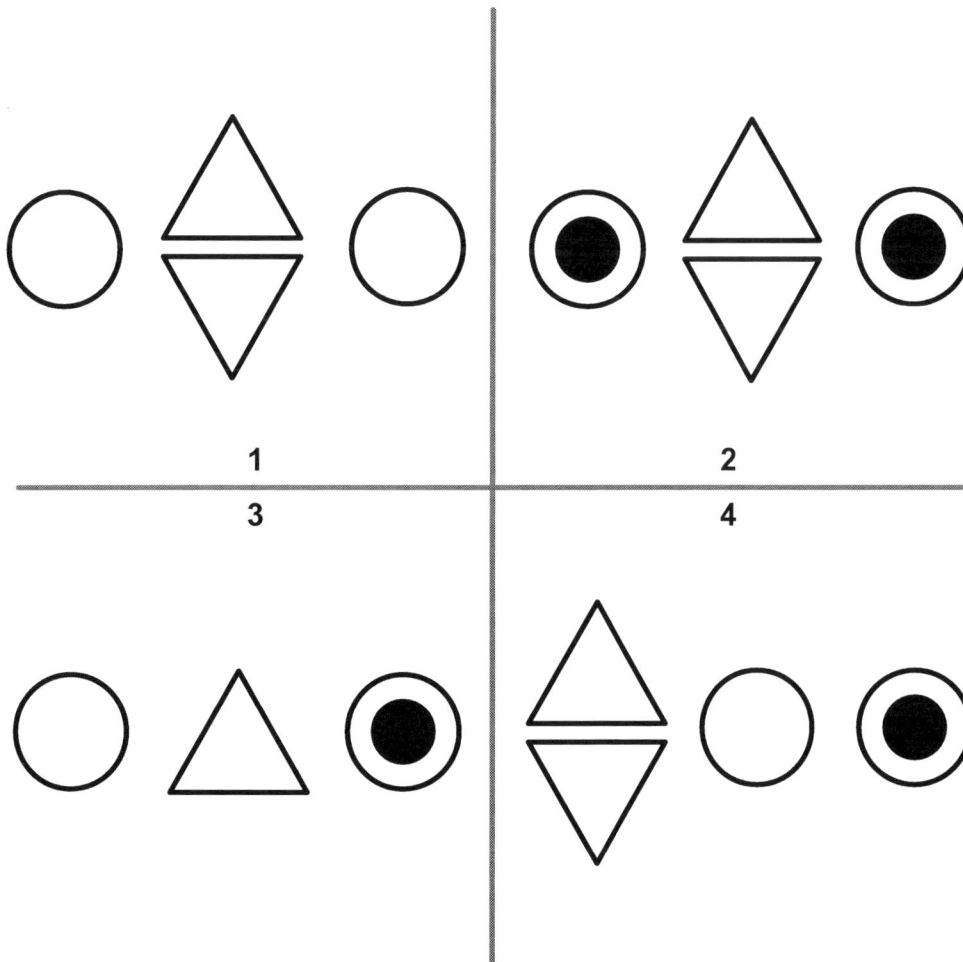

1

2

3

4

FOLLOWING DIRECTIONS

16. Look at the four pictures.

Level 1: Point to the picture where the first jar is empty.
Level 2: Point to the picture that shows a full jar of beans followed by an empty jar.
Level 3: Point to the picture that shows a half-full jar of beans that are in between an empty jar and a full jar.

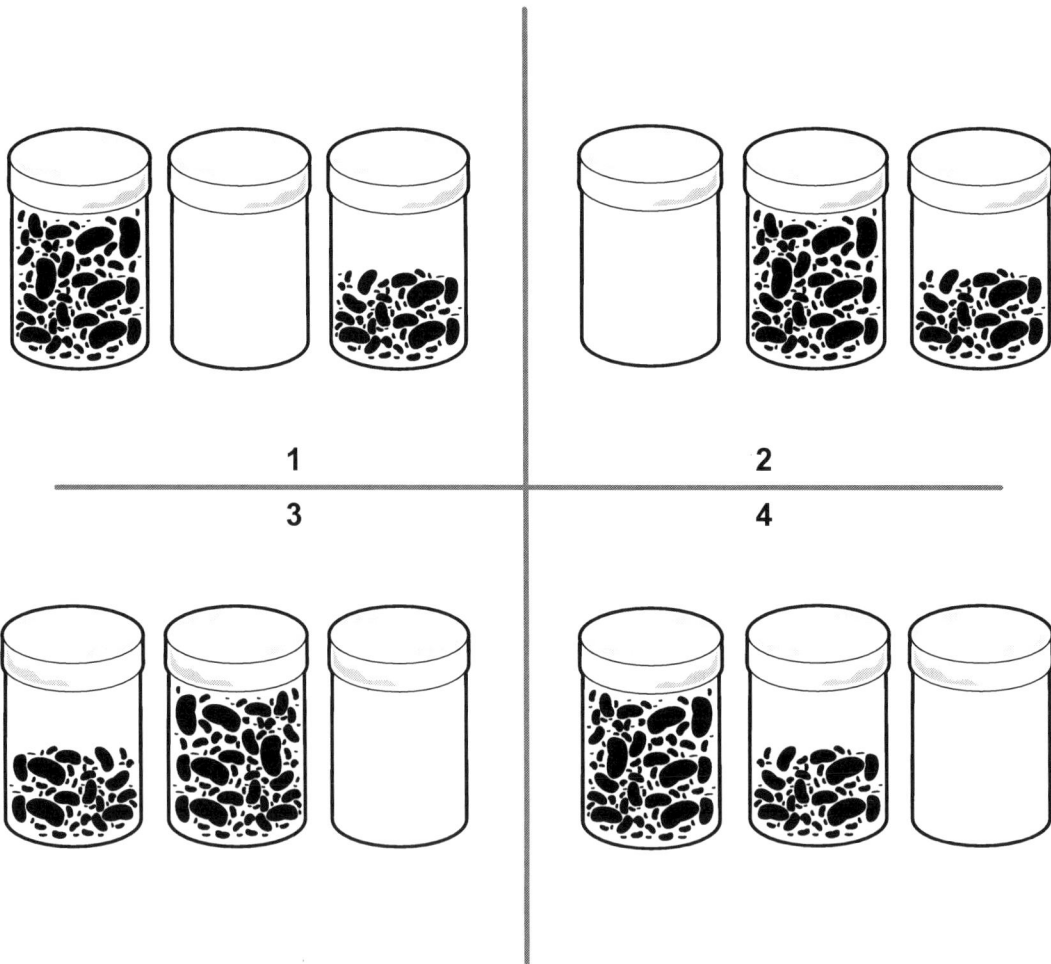

1

2

3

4

112   **Following Directions and Aural Reasoning**   Bright Kids NYC Inc ©

17. Look at the four pictures.

Level 1: Point to the picture where the first letter is the "Z".

Level 2: Point to the picture where the letter "A" is immediately followed by "Z" and "C".

Level 3: Point to the picture where the letters "B" and "Z" are in between the letters "A" and "C".

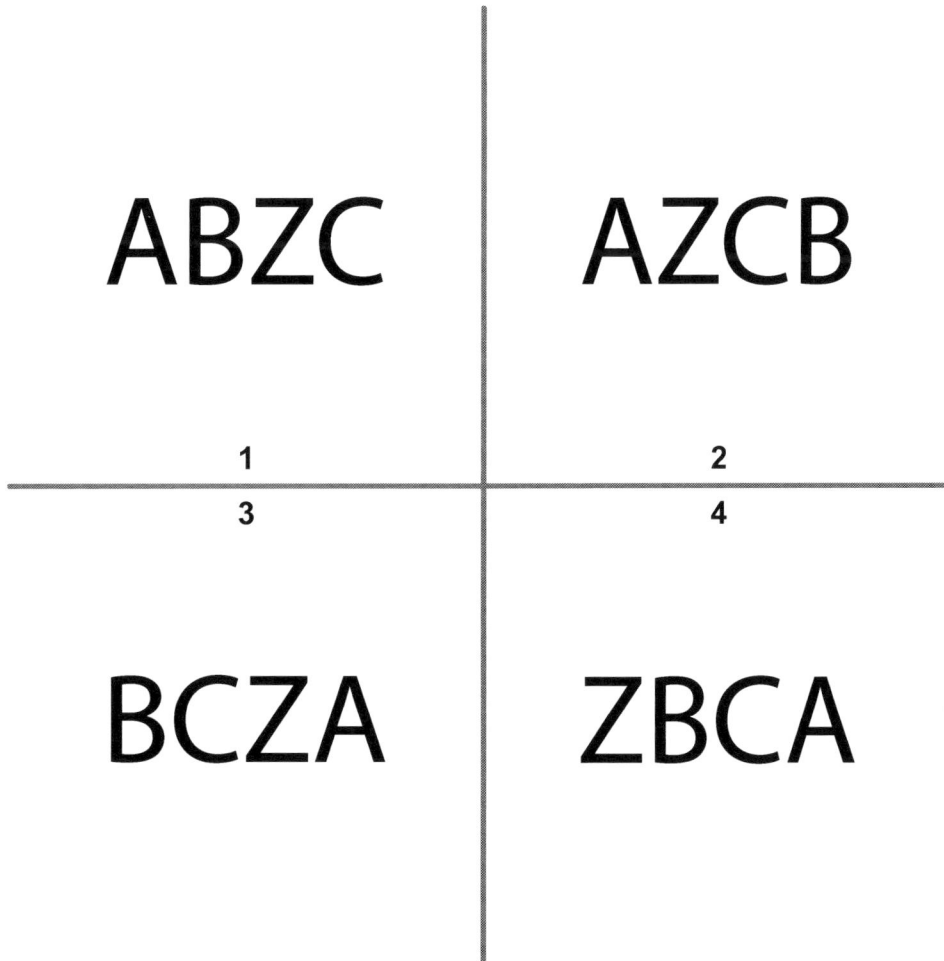

ABZC	AZCB
1	2
3	4
BCZA	ZBCA

18. Look at the four pictures.

Level 1: Point to the picture that has two white squares.

Level 2: Point to the picture that has two gray circles that are above a white square and a gray square.

Level 3: Point to the picture that has one gray circle that is next to a white circle and is on top of a white square.

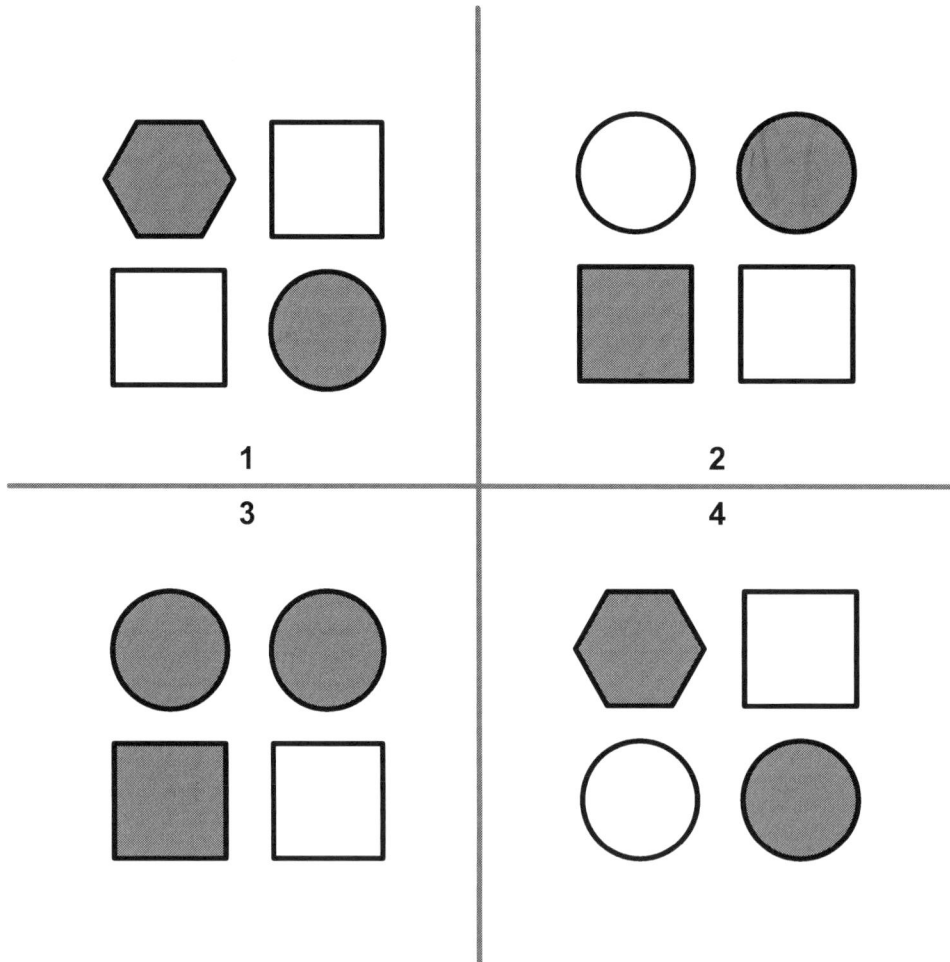

1

2

3

4

19. Look at the chart with numbers, letters and shapes in it.

Level 1: Point to the letter above the number "5".
Level 2: Point to the letter to the right of a black circle.
Level 3: Point to the letter that is to the left of the letter "B" and is above the number "5".

20. **Look at the four pictures.**

Level 1: Point to the picture where the last shape is a black circle.

Level 2: Point to the picture that shows a black shape that is in between two white shapes.

Level 3: Point to the picture that shows a white circle that is in between a black parallelogram and a gray triangle.

1

2

3

4

21. **Look at the four pictures.**

Level 1: Point to the picture that shows three straight lines.
Level 2: Point to the picture that shows a straight line in between two zigzag lines.
Level 3: Point to the picture that shows two zigzag lines that are in between two straight lines.

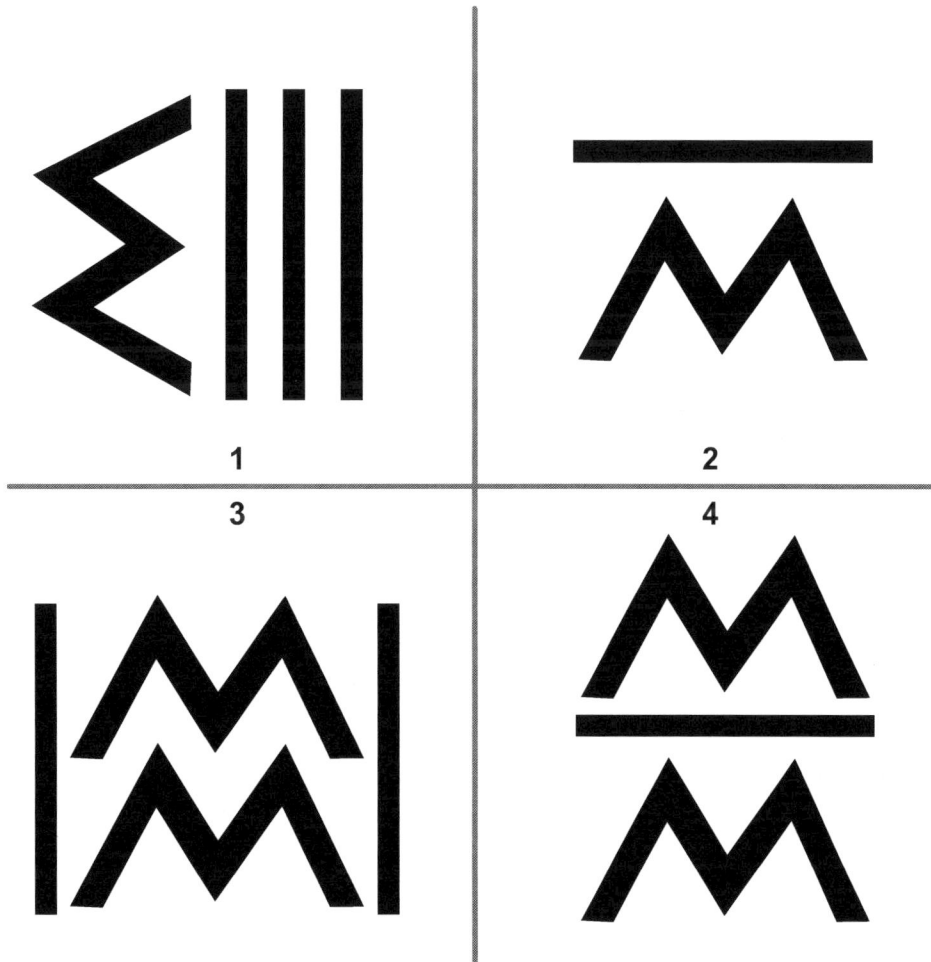

1   2

3   4

22. **Look at the four pictures.**

Level 1: Point to the picture that only shows two birds.

Level 2: Point to the picture that only shows two white birds on top of the fence.

Level 3: Point to the picture that shows one gray bird below the white birds.

1

2

3

4

23. Look at the four pictures.

Level 1: Point to the picture that shows an arrow pointing to the letter "N".
Level 2: Point to the picture that shows arrows pointing to the numbers "2" and "4".
Level 3: Point to the picture that shows arrows pointing to the number "5" and the letters "X" and "A".

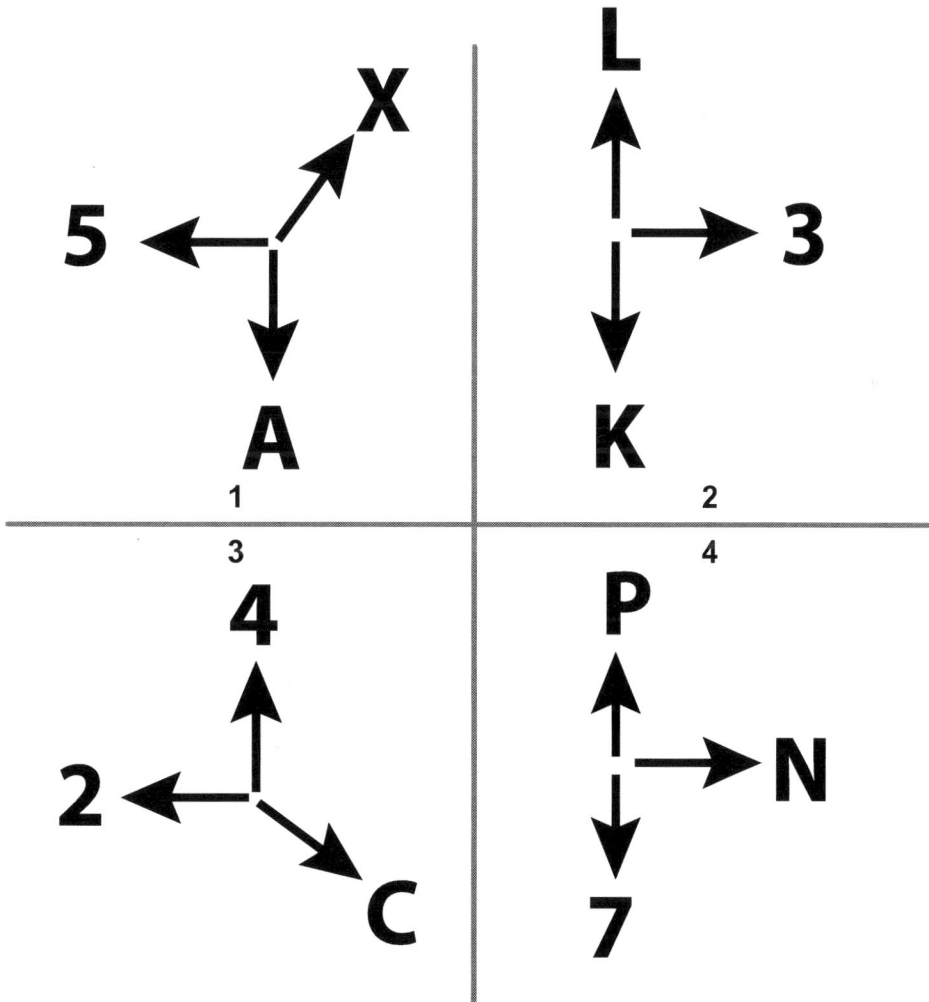

24. Look at the four pictures.

Level 1: Point to the picture that only shows two cats.
Level 2: Point to the picture that only shows a pair of cats and a dog.
Level 3: Point to the picture that shows a dog and three different types of cats.

1   2

3   4

25. Look at the charts below.

Level 1: Point to the picture where the letters "B" and "D" have traded places.
Level 2: Point to the picture where the letter "B" has traded places with the letter "L" and the letter "M" has traded places with the letter "D".
Level 3: Point to the picture where the letters "L" and "M" first trade places and then the letter "M" trades places with the letter "B".

B	L
M	D

L	B		D	L
D	M		M	B

1   2

3   4

D	M		M	B
B	L		L	D

26. **Look at the four pictures.**

Level 1: Point to the picture that has a small white square next to a small black triangle.

Level 2: Point to the picture that has a big black triangle in between a small white circle and a small white triangle.

Level 3: Point to the picture that starts with a big white square and ends with a small white square.

1

2

3

4

27. Look at the four pictures.

Level 1: Point to the picture where the letter "B" is on top.

Level 2: Point to the picture where the letter "C" is in between the letters "D" and "B".

Level 3: Point to the picture where the letter "B" is below the letter "D" and is on top of the letter "C".

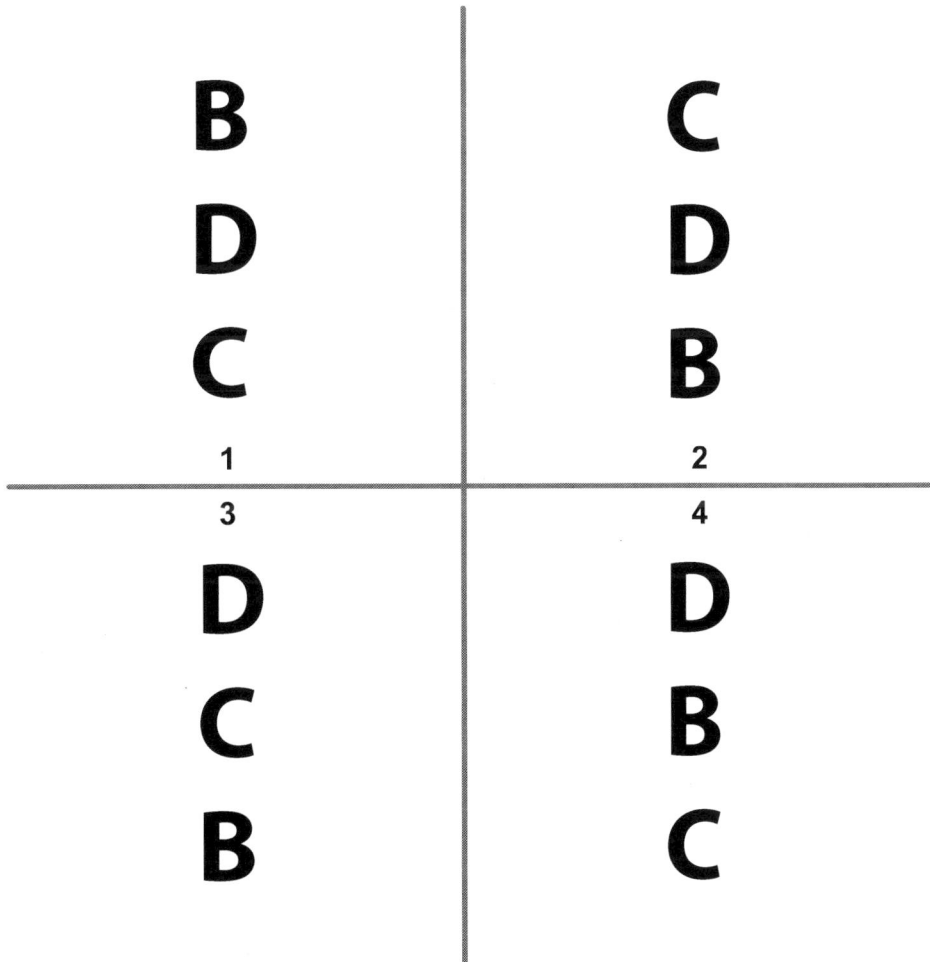

28. Look at the letter blocks below.

Level 1: Point to the group of letter blocks that begin with the letter "R".

Level 2: Point to the group of letter blocks where the letter blocks "M" and "Y" have traded places.

Level 3: Point to the group of letter blocks where all of the letter blocks have traded places with each other.

1

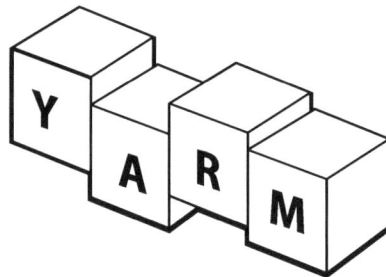

2

3

4

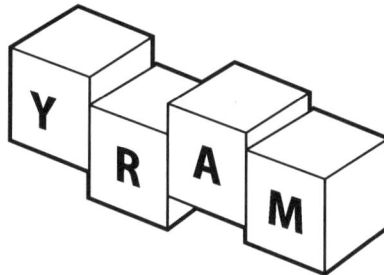

29. Look at the four pictures.

Level 1: Point to the picture that shows three different shapes.
Level 2: Point to the picture that shows two triangles that are next to each other.
Level 3: Point to the picture that shows a large square in between two small triangles.

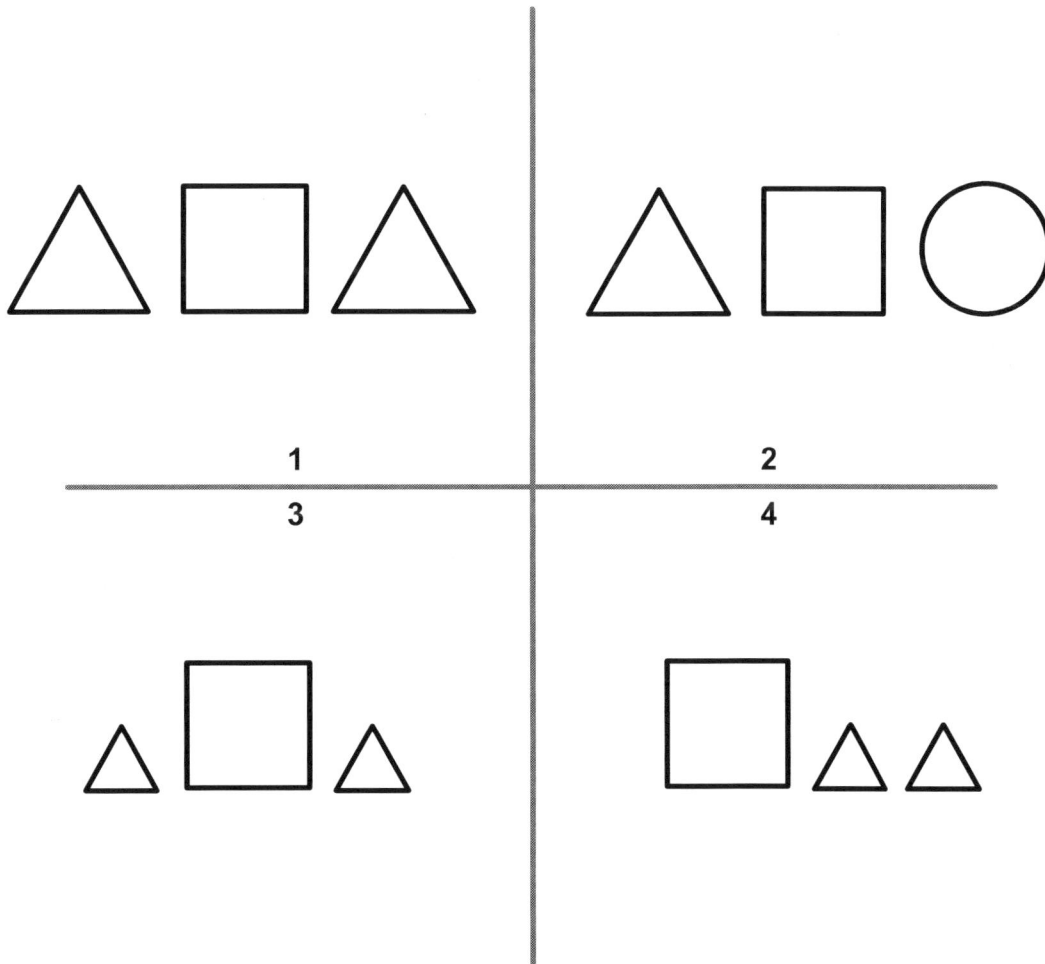

30. Look at the four pictures.

Level 1: Point to the picture that shows two empty bowls that are side by side.
Level 2: Point to the picture that shows two full bowls and one empty bowl.
Level 3: Point to the picture that shows a full bowl that is in between two half-full bowls.

1

2

3

4

Chapter Six

Aural Reasoning

04. Clara did her laundry and none of her clothes came out clean. Mark under the picture that shows Clara's laundry.

① ② ③ ④

05. Lorraine wanted to play outside on a cold winter day. When she came back inside, her hands were freezing. Mark under the picture that shows what Lorraine forgot to put on before she went outside on a cold day.

① ② ③ ④

06. Ellen was making a milkshake. First, she got all the ingredients ready and put them next to the blender. Second, she blended everything. After that, she put some ice cubes in her milkshake. Finally she drank the milkshake. Mark under the picture that shows what Ellen did first.

① ② ③ ④

01. Alan wanted to paint his new doghouse. Mark under the picture that shows [what he] needs to paint his doghouse.

① ② ③

02. Paul went to the library and took his book, backpack and hat. He l[eft] under the picture that shows what Paul had at the library.

① ② ③

03. Monica had one striped cat, one gray cat and one black cat. Finn also had three ca[ts] not have any gray cats. Mark under the picture that shows Finn's cats.

① ② ③ ④

Following Directions and Aural Reasoning

Bright Kids NYC Inc ©

01. Alan wanted to paint his new doghouse. Mark under the picture that shows the two things Alan needs to paint his doghouse.

         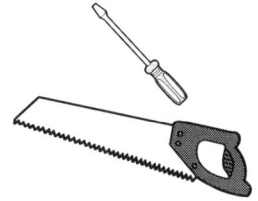

   ①   ②   ③   ④

02. Paul went to the library and took his book, backpack and hat. He lost his hat on the way. Mark under the picture that shows what Paul had he reached the library.

   ①   ②   ③   ④

03. Monica had one striped cat, one gray cat, and one black cat. Finn also had three cats, but he did not have any gray cats. Mark under the picture that shows Finn's cats.

   ①   ②   ③   ④

04. Clara did her laundry and none of her clothes came out clean. Mark under the picture that shows Clara's laundry.

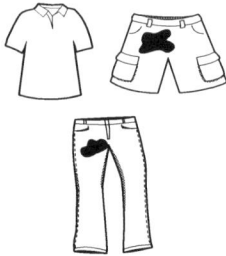  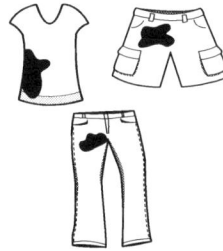 

      ①   ②   ③   ④

05. Lorraine wanted to play outside on a cold winter day. When she came back inside, her hands were freezing. Mark under the picture that shows what Lorraine forgot to put on before she went outside on a cold day.

  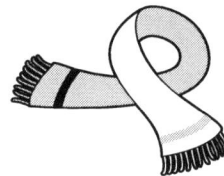 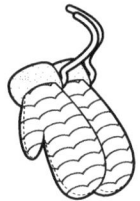

      ①   ②   ③   ④

06. Ellen was making a milkshake. First, she got all the ingredients ready and put them next to the blender. Second, she blended everything. After that, she put some ice cubes in her milkshake. Finally, she drank the milkshake. Mark under the picture that shows what Ellen did first.

      ①   ②   ③   ④

07. Jody's mother wanted to prepare a plate of fruit for Jody. Jody said, "I only want to eat berries and bananas." Mark under the picture of the fruit plate that Jody's mother prepared for Jody.

　　　① 　　　　　② 　　　　　③ 　　　　　④

08. Mark's teacher gave each student a piece of paper to draw on. She said, "Before you begin, write your entire name in lowercase letters on the top middle part of your paper." Mark under the picture where Mark correctly followed the teacher's instructions.

 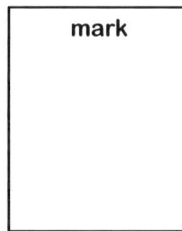 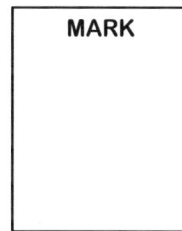 

　　　① 　　　　　② 　　　　　③ 　　　　　④

09. Mark under the picture that shows this: There is something to eat, something to read, and something to write with.

　　　① 　　　　　② 　　　　　③ 　　　　　④

10. Emily is the tallest child in her family. When Emily and her brothers stand in line to buy popcorn, Emily is always in the middle. Mark under the picture that shows what Emily's siblings look like when they line up to buy ice cream.

① ② ③ ④

---

11. When Jake came home from baseball practice, he was so tired that he dozed off before bedtime. Mark under the picture that shows what Jake did after he came home from baseball practice.

① ② ③ ④

---

12. Melissa has to wear a uniform to her new school every day. Her uniform is all white, except for the collar and the skirt. Mark under the picture that shows Melissa's uniform.

① ② ③ ④

13. Kate wanted to eat something to keep her warm on a cold winter day. Mark under the picture of the food that Kate ate on a cold winter day.

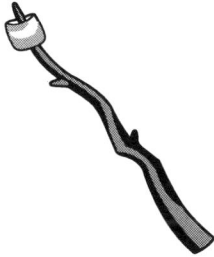 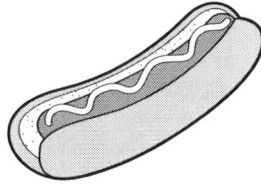  

       ①   ②   ③   ④

14. David planted two seeds in his flower pot. Then, he gave the flower pot to his neighbor to take care of before he left for his vacation. Mark under the picture that shows what David's flower pot looked like when he returned home from his vacation and retrieved the flower pot from his neighbor.

       ①   ②   ③   ④

15. Kathleen and her brother Chris were playing baseball. Chris threw the baseball to Kathleen when she wasn't looking. Mark under the picture that shows what might have happened while Kathleen and her brother were playing baseball.

       ①   ②   ③   ④

16. Matilda and Darius built a snowman. They put everything on the snowman except for the arms. Mark under the picture that shows what the snowman looked like after a few days of sunny weather.

①   ②   ③   ④

17. Megan lost her favorite toy at the beach. Mark under the picture that shows what Megan did after she lost her favorite toy at the beach.

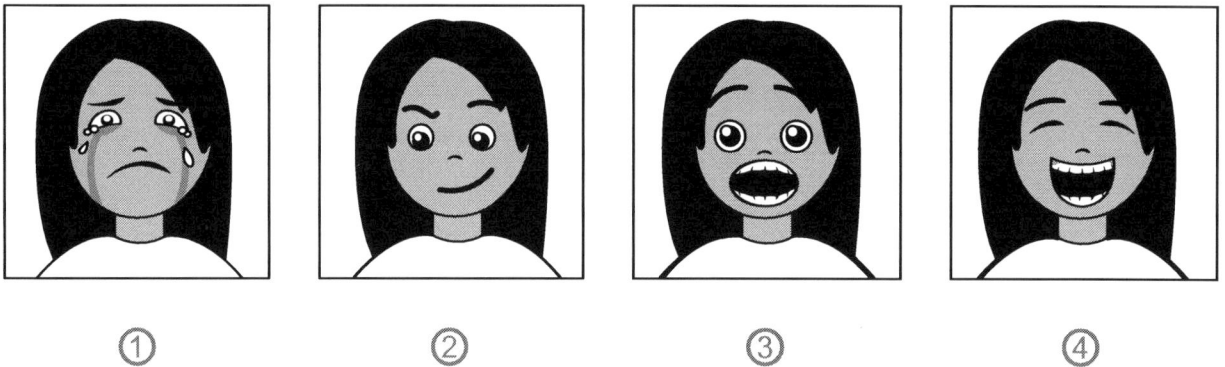

①   ②   ③   ④

18. Frank's mother wanted him to pick up all of the fallen leaves outside their house before the Halloween party. Mark under the picture of the item that Frank used to pick up the leaves.

①   ②   ③   ④

19. Isabella had a sore throat and needed something to keep her warm. Mark under the picture of the item that Isabella needed to keep warm.

①   ②   ③   ④

20. Joshua was hungry at the fair. He bought something to eat, but he couldn't bite into it because he thought it was too cold. Mark under the picture of the food that Joshua thought was too cold to bite into.

  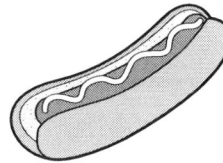 

①   ②   ③   ④

21. Sofia ate two cookies and a cupcake for a snack at a party. Mary ate the same thing, except she didn't eat a cupcake. Mark under the picture that shows what Mary ate at the party.

 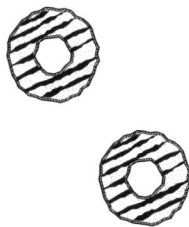  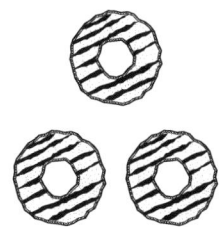

①   ②   ③   ④

22. Lucas opened his backpack and realized that he had twice as many pens as pencils. Mark under the picture that shows what Lucas had in his backpack.

①   ②   ③   ④

23. Nicole was going on vacation. Her mother said, "You can bring anything you want to wear, but make sure to pack at least two pairs of pants and two shirts." Mark under the picture that shows what Nicole packed.

         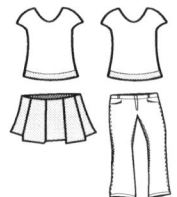

①   ②   ③   ④

24. Jason always goes to the beach with something that he can eat, something that can help him see underwater, and something that can dry him after he's done swimming. Mark under the picture of the items that Jason most likely brings to the beach.

   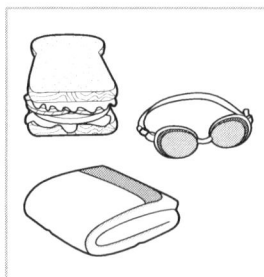      

①   ②   ③   ④

25. Tim and Sean wanted to hang a painting on the wall. Mark under the picture of the tools that Tim and Sean will need to hang the painting on the wall.

     ①   ②   ③   ④

26. Brian and Jessica baked a birthday cake for their mother. Before they were finished baking the cake, they had to go to the store to buy another cake. Mark under the picture that shows what might have happened to the cake they were trying to bake.

     ①   ②   ③   ④

27. Claudia was excited about her special breakfast this morning. She said, "I need some syrup for my special breakfast." Mark under the picture that shows what Claudia was about to have for breakfast.

     ①   ②   ③   ④

28. Cyrus' mother wanted him to measure all of the pieces of wood that he wanted before he cut them for the treehouse he was making. Mark under the picture of the item that Cyrus used to measure the pieces of wood.

①   ②   ③   ④

29. Andrew was playing in the woods when his mother shouted, "Be careful! That insect can sting!" Mark under the picture that shows the insect that Andrew's mother was shouting about.

      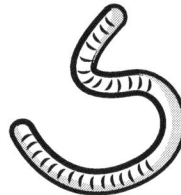   

①   ②   ③   ④

30. Linda's mother made a lot of cupcakes for her birthday party. Mark under the picture of the type of cupcake that Linda and her friends tried and liked the least.

         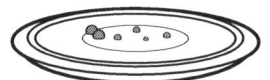

①   ②   ③   ④

Answer Keys

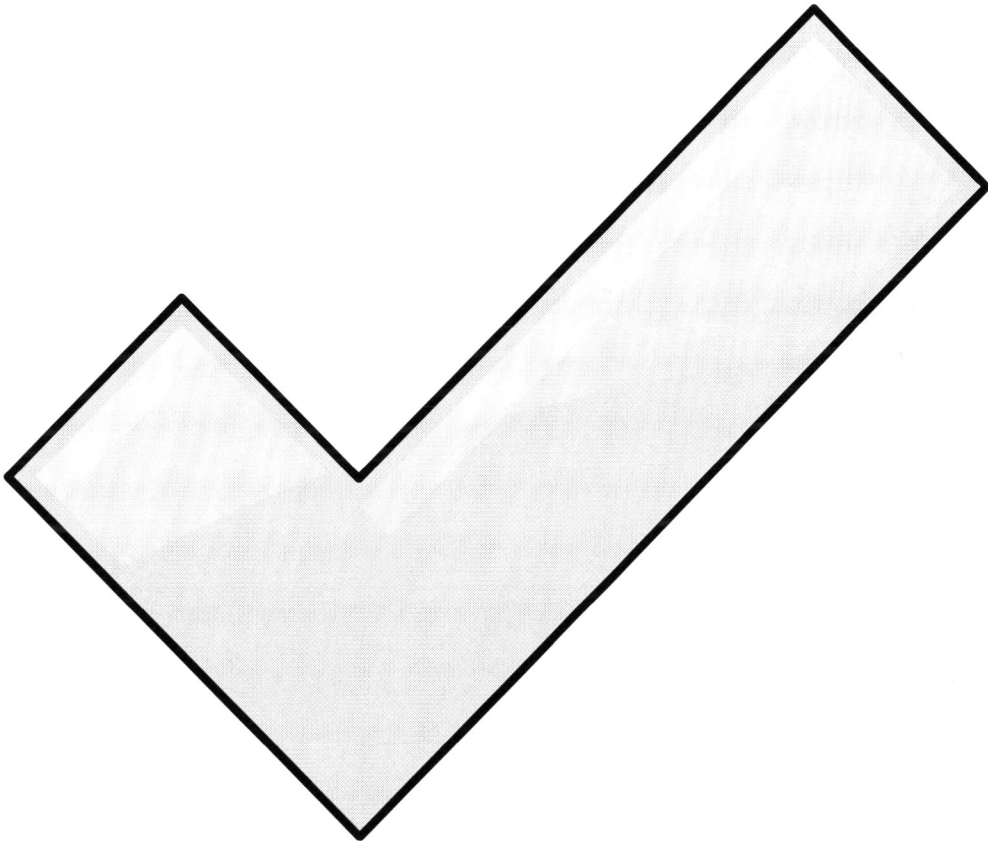

Following Directions and Aural Reasoning

Bright Kids NYC Inc ©

Skill Builder Activities

Page 15

Page 16

Page 17

Page 18

Page 19

Page 20

Page 21

Page 22

Page 23

Skill Builder Activities - Riddles

Page 24

Page 27

Page 28

Page 29

Page 30

Page 31

Page 32

Page 33

Page 34

Skill Builder Activities - Riddles

Page 35

Page 36

Page 37

Page 38

Page 39

Page 40

Page 41

Page 42

Page 43

Skill Builder Activities - Riddles

Page 44

SKILL BUILDER ACTIVITIES - RIDDLES

18. I'm quite a bit different from these other three.

See how they are alike, then you will find me.

Of the pictures that you see, which one is me?

Page 45

SKILL BUILDER ACTIVITIES - RIDDLES

19. I love pumpkins in the fall.

Mine is the scariest of them all.

Of the pictures you see, which pumpkin is for me?

Page 46

SKILL BUILDER ACTIVITIES - RIDDLES

20. The musical instrument I like to play,

has no strings or keys in any way.

Of the pictures you see, which one instrument is for me?

Page 47

SKILL BUILDER ACTIVITIES - RIDDLES

21. My house is green and the garage is blue.

I have a car that's old and a car that's new.

Of the pictures that you see, which one is me?

Page 48

SKILL BUILDER ACTIVITIES - RIDDLES

22. In the air I'm usually found,

especially since I don't run fast on the ground.

Of the pictures that you see, which one is me?

Page 49

SKILL BUILDER ACTIVITIES - RIDDLES

23. Black and white, behind the tree,

when I get scared, it gets smelly.

Of the pictures that you see, which one is me?

Page 50

SKILL BUILDER ACTIVITIES - RIDDLES

24. A green frog ate a black ant.

A spotted snake ate the green frog.

A tiger ate the spotted snake, black ant, and green frog.

Of the pictures that you see, who is left in this story?

Page 51

SKILL BUILDER ACTIVITIES - RIDDLES

25. May entered a pizza eating contest.

She ate half of a pizza and then left the rest.

In front of her seat, which pizza did May eat?

Page 52

SKILL BUILDER ACTIVITIES - RIDDLES

28. I am a boy who is short,

whose wearing a yellow hat and a blue coat.

Of the pictures you see, which one is me?

Skill Builder Activities - Riddles

Page 53

Page 54

Page 55

Page 56

Aural Directions

Page 78

Page 79

Page 80

Following Directions, Pages 95-126

1. Level 1: **1**, Level 2: **4**, Level 3: **3**

2. Level 1: **4**, Level 2: **1**, Level 3: **3**

3. Level 1: **1**, Level 2: **3**, Level 3: **4**

4. Level 1: **4**, Level 2: **3**, Level 3: **2**

5. Level 1: **4**, Level 2: **2**, Level 3: **3**

6. Level 1: **1**, Level 2: **4**, Level 3: **3**

7. Level 1: **3**, Level 2: **4**, Level 3: **1**

8. Level 1: **2**, Level 2: **3**, Level 3: **4**

9. Level 1: **1**, Level 2: **4**, Level 3: **2**

10. Level 1: **3**, Level 2: **4**, Level 3: **2**

11. Level 1: **3**, Level 2: **4**, Level 3: **2**

12. Level 1: **2**, Level 2: **4**, Level 3: **1**

13. Level 1: **2**, Level 2: **4**, Level 3: **3**

14. Level 1: **4**, Level 2: **6**, Level 3: **1**

15. Level 1: **3**, Level 2: **2**, Level 3: **4**

16. Level 1: **2**, Level 2: **1**, Level 3: **4**

17. Level 1: **4**, Level 2: **2**, Level 3: **1**

18. Level 1: **1**, Level 2: **3**, Level 3: **2**

19. Level 1: **A**, Level 2: **K**, Level 3: **A**

20. Level 1: **1**, Level 2: **3**, Level 3: **2**

21. Level 1: **1**, Level 2: **4**, Level 3: **3**

22. Level 1: **1**, Level 2: **2**, Level 3: **4**

23. Level 1: **4**, Level 2: **3**, Level 3: **1**

24. Level 1: **2**, Level 2: **3**, Level 3: **4**

25. Level 1: **2**, Level 2: **1**, Level 3: **4**

26. Level 1: **4**, Level 2: **3**, Level 3: **1**

27. Level 1: **1**, Level 2: **3**, Level 3: **4**

28. Level 1: **1**, Level 2: **2**, Level 3: **4**

29. Level 1: **2**, Level 2: **4**, Level 3: **3**

30. Level 1: **1**, Level 2: **2**, Level 3: **4**

Aural Reasoning, Pages 127-138

1. 1	16. 3
2. 3	17. 1
3. 3	18. 4
4. 3	19. 2
5. 4	20. 1
6. 2	21. 2
7. 2	22. 1
8. 2	23. 3
9. 1	24. 2
10. 2	25. 1
11. 3	26. 4
12. 4	27. 3
13. 3	28. 3
14. 4	29. 4
15. 1	30. 3

Following Directions and Aural Reasoning

Bright Kids NYC Inc ©